Michelangelo's *Pietà* in St. Peter's Basilica, Vatican City

---
1   *http://en.wikpedia.org/wiki/File:Michelangelo's_*Pieta_5450_cropncleaned

Our Tenacity of Faith

America's Catholic Heritage

By
Ann M. Casey

For beginnings, the study of history contains all the specific ordinary starting and ending points, their requirement only in a linear regimen. Catholicism, rather than being impeded by those structural limitations, gathers and garners times and periods for access to reconstruct the understanding of each generation to bring its past to the next generation. "Tend my flock" and with that, "Who hears you, hears me," the first import of the request insured the continual and constant stability of the Catholic faith in her Church. Ordained by God and given in sacrifice for humanity's humbleness of birth, an infant assumed and placed on His shoulders the sins committed by man, yet with the absolute promise of salvation. This is our living and vibrant legacy of the Catholic Church and within all lies our capability of carrying the banner for God and resisting the culpability of conquest for riches to fill the impoverished coffers of kings.

Ordinary men ordained by God took the call to become missionaries and travelled with those, in America's beginnings to spread the faith and prevent the excesses of greed and the superiority of Europe with their due right of conqueror. For the temptations were great, for shortly after Columbus planted the cross in the Bahamas, His Holy Father Pope Alexander VI awarded sole colonial rights over most of the New World to Spain in the firm intention of spreading God's word. Yet with the lure of treasures lying before them, the Conquistadors gave sway to their baser instincts and thereby giving the native population little credence for belief in the white man's God when the Franciscans came to teach the catechism after the arrival of Cortes. The consequences for the missionaries were proved on two points, by Cortes' decision to leave Pedro de Alvarado in charge during his absence, and also when Charles V, who by granting Don Nuno de Guzman as a ruler over the native population, flaunted his authority with cruel and vindictive measures. As a result, the native inhabitants viewed that there was little difference between conqueror and religious.

In later years, when the Jesuits carried the cross, they heeded well to what Father Paul Rogueneau wrote in 1647, this carried the philosophy of the Jesuits from the beginning.

> *'One must be very careful before condemning a thousand things and customs, which greatly offends minds brought up and nourished in another world. It is easy to call irreligious what is merely stupidity, and to take for diabolical workings something that is nothing more than human; and then one thinks he is obliged to forbid as impious certain things that are done in all innocence, or, at the most, are silly but not criminal customs.... I have no hesitation in saying that we have been too severe in this point.'* [2]

Notwithstanding, the wars among the various native clans often times imposed its own death sentence to martyrdom. And for here, within the cultural context of each nation coming to the Americas, the conundrums of carrying on the faith first, lax for the most part in the explorers, the riches to be had become the spoiler for the dreams in immediate acquisition and mitigating the inroads made by the priests, tragedy was the result. Yet, within the play of political demand of each country – the Catholic Church was without the boundaries by the nationalistic fervor that was commandeering state over church in the sixteenth century.

From the Catechism of the Catholic Church

'Whoever teaches must become all things to men.'

(I Cor 9:22)

---

[2] Paul Rogueneau 1647, The Jesuit Relations

'Above all, teachers must not imagine that a single kind of soul has been entrusted to them, and that consequently it is lawfull to teach and form all the faithful in true piety with one and the same method! Let them realize that some are in Christ as newborn babes, other are adolescents, and still others as adults in full command of their powers.... Those who are called to the ministry of preaching must suit their words to the maturity and understanding of their hearers as they hand on the teaching of the mysteries of faith and the rules of moral conduct."

Roman Catechism Preface: - 10: 1 Cor 13:8

"The whole concern of doctrine and its teaching must be directed to the love that never ends. Whether something is proposed for belief, for hope or for action, the love of our Lord must always be made accessible, so that anyone can see that all the works of perfect Christian virtue spring from love and have no other objective than to arrive at love."

TABLE OF CONTENTS

5   CHAPTER ONE:
THE FAITH FROM THE SOUTH:
SPANISH TERRITORIES, MISSIONARIES

    Mexico's Conquest   8
    Our Lady of Guadalupe   8

15 CHAPTER TWO:
FLORIDA'S MISSIONS: 1565-1700

    The Georgia Martyrs   18
    The Guale Uprising   19
    Guale Uprising Aftermath   22

29 CHAPTER THREE:
THE FAITH FROM THE NORTH: FRENCH TERRITORIES,
MISSIONARIES THE JESUIT MARTYRS

    Martyrdom of Rene' Goupil   38
    Martyrdom of Father Issac Jogues   40
    Martyrdom of Father Antony Daniel   41
    Martyrdom of Fathers Brébeuf and Lalemant   42
    Martyrdom of Fathers Garnier and Chabanel   44
    Let Us Pray   46

49 **CHAPTER FOUR:**
   BLESSED KATERI TEKAKWITHA 1656-1680

57 **CHAPTER FIVE:**
   FAITH FROM ENGLAND: 1600-1634
     THE CONCEPTION OF THE MARYLAND COLONY

67 **CHAPTER SIX:**
   THE LIFE OF THE MARYLAND COLONY 1634-1769

83 **CHAPTER SEVEN:**
   THE REVOLUTIONARY WAR CATHOLICS

97 **CHAPTER EIGHT:**
   THE MISSIONS AND CATHOLIC EDUCATION 1600-1860

      The missionary martyrs   106

113 **CHAPTER NINE:**
   ARCHBISHOP CARROLL AND SAINT MOTHER SETON

131 **CHAPTER TEN:**
   ANTI-CATHOLIC RIOTS IN THE NINETEENTH CENTURY

151 INDEX

Chapter One:
The Faith from the South: Spanish Territories, Missionaries

Missionaries and Our Lady of Guadalupe

Regardless of tumultuous events, Catholicism has permeated into our very bones with a knowledge at once so great and simple, that we remain content to the future, yet distressed, our earthly sojourn carries little of the strength Calvary necessitated by example. Though within our soul's search, we have the solace and joy of the many of those who preceded our footsteps in keeping the lantern lit. Our small burdens are not shouldered in vain, but have the quality of the tangible to reach and grasp for the intangible.

Europe's ventures into the Americas is credited first, at least through legend, by Saint Brendan of Ireland to the shores of Maine four hundred years prior to Columbus' exploration of a route to the Indies. Saint Brendan, though quite the traveler brought many to the faith in Ireland and Scotland, did not bring souls to the Catholic Church in the Americas. Columbus' voyages and discoveries are verified however and brought about the great conquest of territory for Spain and for the Catholic Church, many souls.

Sixteenth Europe's causes of expansion to the New World does little to deepen one's understanding of the empathetic knowledge of the purpose God placed in the hands of Catholic missionaries and their certainty to accept the path He would lead them on.

Infallible Papal authority was and is the Divine authority over kings and nations. From the Chair of Peter, all moral teaching, interpretation and governing souls and salvation is accorded to the Pope as Christ's apostle on earth. From the papal decrees and Bulls regarding the expansion of territory, exploration and with it, the establishing of Catholicism was and is the sole right of the Pope. The hierarchy of God first through the Pope and second for the King's governance was the force, which maintained absolute authority over man. Under this banner in 1493 Alexander VI's, Inter caetera granted Spain sole colonial rights of exploration and the establishment of Catholicism in the New World. The tip of Brazil was granted to Portugal.

At the time all Europe was Catholic and in that therein lay the conflicts. Spain's recent victory over the Ottoman Empire empowered her to explore and conquer the New World. The king's coffers of England and France were depleted from the wars and even Rome had been sacked. The necessity of replenishment was surely to be found in the conquest and domination of new territory, but for all that, the banner of the cross was sailed under first.

The difficulty lies in reconciling how the ruling of man skewed often times the touch of God. Yet in Mass, we see, hear and know their names, their commitment, their viewpoint and steadfast belief was salvation and not the torture of slavery that modern history's accusers have leveled against them. Be cognizant of the time period and the civilization the early explorers left behind to venture willingly for Christ's request. On arrival to the new world, its culture was incomprehensible to their own way of life.

Prior to the arrival of Cortez on Good Friday in 1519, the Aztecs ruled most of Central America, Mexico, and south through portions of Honduras and El Salvador. In stark contrast to Catholicism, the religious practices of the Aztecs had greater cause for scrutiny than other tribal clans of the area. The Aztecs believed their gods required human blood to subsist and their priests gladly sacrificed thousands of living humans to stay appeased from the wrath of their deities. The unfortunate victims were not the Aztecs themselves, but captured Indians from the surrounding tribes. The names of the gods they worshipped were the Quetzalcoatl, the feathered serpent, who founded the Aztec nation, but left when human sacrifice began, opposing the horrific ritual, yet vowed to return and redeem his people in the year of 1 reed, which in the Aztec calendar occurred every 52 years. Tonantzin was the mother god, and she of the two was the more terrifying, her head comprising of snakes and her garment, a mass of writhing serpents, and her eyes projected a fathomless grief. She was worshipped at a stone temple in Tepeyac', where on December 9th of 1531 twelve years later, the Virgin Mary first appeared to Juan Diego.

Two events occurred that some may refer to as coincidence, while others reference as part of the divine plan. 1) The year of Quetzalcoatl's return coincided with Cortez's arrival under Catholic Spain's banner and 2) the time of the Virgin Mary's appearance with the imminent insurrection of the native population against Spanish rule. As the Aztecs had dominated the surrounding tribes, so too did the Don Nuno de Guzman in his cruel and ruthless treatment to the Indians. Nuno de Guzman was a Spanish conquistador and bodyguard to King Charles V who appointed him as colonial administrator of New Spain. Later he was sent by King Charles to counterbalance the influence of Hernan Cortes, as the King worried Cortes was becoming too powerful.

Mexico's Conquest

In the year 1528, King Charles -V of Spain appointed the administration of five governors to oversee Mexico, also appointing at the time Friar Juan de Zumarraga as the first Bishop of Mexico City and Protector of the Indians. (In his 25 years as Bishop, he established the first grammar school, library, printing press, and the first college, *Colegio de la Santa Cruz* at Tlatelolco. One of the first teachers at the College was the Franciscan Fray Bernardino de Sahagún, author of the Florentine Codex, a study of the Aztec Náhuatl language and culture.) Though his first year as Bishop was spent in a constant objection to Nuno de Guzman's cruel and merciless treatment of the Indians whom he had to date sold 15,000 into slavery. Even though strict censorship measures were in place and both Indians and Spaniards were forbidden from bringing complaints to the Bishop, a smuggled message did gain access to Bishop Zumarraga who in turn smuggled a message hidden in a crucifix back to Spain. Nuno de Guzman was recalled to Spain and a new council was set up, but their arrival did not occur until 1531.

Our Lady of Guadalupe

Perhaps the prayers of Bishop Zumarraga were heard, though not quite to the extent that he could ever imagine, for on December 9th, 1531, our Lady appeared to an Aztec convert named Juan Diego on his way to early morning Mass. She called to him in his language and his native name.

> "Juan Diego!" The young woman said: "Dear little son, I love you. I want you to know who I am. "I am the Virgin Mary, Mother of the one true God, of Him who gives life. He is Lord and Creator of heaven and of earth. I desire that there be built a temple at this place where I want to manifest Him, make him known, give Him to all people through my love, my compassion, my help, and my protection. I truly am your merciful Mother, your Mother and the Mother of all who dwell in this land, and of all mankind, of all those who love me, of those who cry to me, and of those who seek and place their trust in me. Here I shall listen to their weeping and their sorrows. I shall take them all to my heart, and I shall cure their many sufferings, afflictions, and sorrows. So run now to Tenochtitlan and tell the Lord Bishop all that you have seen and heard."

At the Bishop's door, Juan was greeted with derision by the servants and when allowed to see the Bishop, was given a gentle disbelief with only a 'Allow me to consider Her words, but pray come visit again.'

Juan returned to find Mary waiting and said to Her, 'Please send someone else who is more suitable to deliver the message, for I am no one.'

She answered his doubts by saying,

> "Listen, little son. There are many I could send. But you are the one I have chosen for this task. So, tomorrow morning, go back to the Bishop. Tell him it is the ever holy Virgin Mary, Mother of God who sends you, and repeat to him my great desire for a church in this place."[3]

Gaining entrance again with the same difficulties, Juan again approached the Bishop, who was surprised to see him again so soon. And now Bishop Zumarraga, disbelieving in the appearance of the Divine, requested a sign for verification. So once again, Juan

---
3   www.maryourmother.net/Guadalupe.html

returned to Our Lady and relayed the Bishop's message. She told Juan to return the following morning and the Bishop will receive his sign.

But at home, Juan found his uncle near death and stayed with him through the night. The next morning he bypassed Tepeyac Hill travelling instead to find his parish priest to give Last Rites to his uncle. The truth was that he was avoiding Mary, but She intercepted his route and blocked his path.

'Mary said, "Least of my sons, what is the matter?"

Juan was embarrassed by her presence, "My Lady, why are you up so early? Are you well? Forgive me. My uncle is dying and desires me to find a priest for the Sacraments. It was no empty promise I made to you yesterday morning. But my uncle fell ill."

Mary said, *"My little son. Do not be distressed and afraid.*

> *Am I not here who is your Mother? Are you not under my shadow and protection?*
>
> *Am I not the fountain of your joy? Are you not in the fold of my mantle, in the cradle of my arms?*
>
> *Your uncle will not die at this time. This very moment his health is restored. There is no reason now for your errand, so you can peacefully attend to mine. Go up to the top of the hill; cut the flowers that are growing there and bring them to me."*

Flowers in December? Impossible, thought Juan Diego. But he was obedient found beautiful Castilian roses on the hilltop. As he cut them, he decided the best way to protect them against the cold was to cradle them in his tilma - a long, cloth cape worn by the Aztecs, and often looped up as a carryall. He ran back to Mary and she rearranged the roses and tied the lower corners of the tilma behind his neck so that nothing would spill, and Mary said,

> *"You see, little son, this is the sign I am sending to the Bishop. Tell him that now he has his sign, he should build the temple I desire in this place. Do not let anyone but him see what you are carrying. Hold both sides until you are in his presence and tell him how I intercepted you on your way to fetch a priest to give the Last Sacraments to your uncle, how I assured you he was perfectly healed and sent you up to cut these roses, and myself arranged them like this. Remember, little son, that you are my trusted ambassador, and this time the Bishop will believe all that you tell him."*

This fourth apparition was the last known time Juan Diego ever saw the Virgin Mary. '

Juan called for the third time on the Bishop and explained all that had passed. Then Juan put up both hands and untied the corners of crude cloth behind his neck. The looped-up fold of the tilma fell; the flowers he thought were the precious sign tumbled out on the floor. The Bishop rose from his chair and fell on his knees in adoration before the tilma, as well as everyone else in the room. For on the tilma was the image of the Blessed Virgin Mary just as described by Juan Diego.[4]

---

4   Saunders, Rev. William. "Saint Juan Diego and Our Lady." *Arlington Catholic*

QUESTIONS

1. You are a Franciscan Monk eager to spread God's word and you see what the soldiers are doing to the native tribes – think and pray in his shoes on what you would do to restrain their base instincts.
2. If you were Bishop Zumarraga, how would you react?
3. If you were Juan Diego, how would you react?
4. Why did at this particular time did Our Lady appear? The history of this event is of prime importance for over 8 million Aztecs converted to the Catholic faith.

---

*Herald catholiceducation.org/articles/**stories**_of_faith_and.../cs0092.htm*

1562, Americae sive quartae orbis partis nova et exactissima descriptio
Map Credit: Courtesy of the Library of Congress, Geography and Map Division.

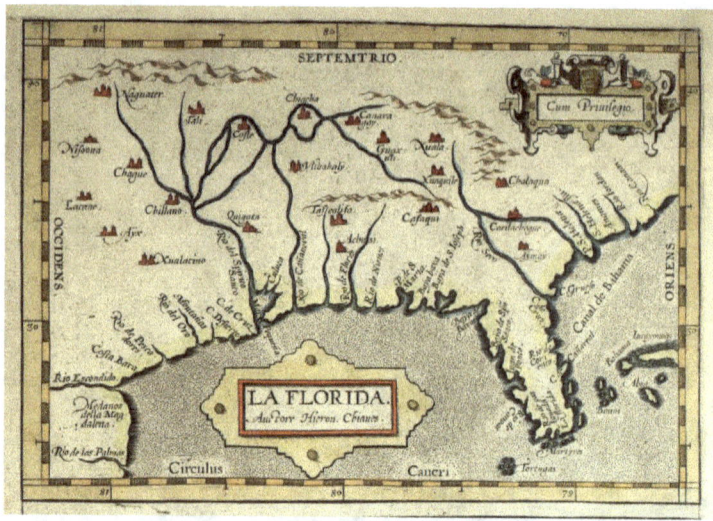

Map drawn of Florida in 1584. The area shown extends throughout the present-day Southeastern United States. Map Credit: Courtesy of the Special Collections Department, University of South Florida. Digitization provided by the USF Libraries Digitization Center.

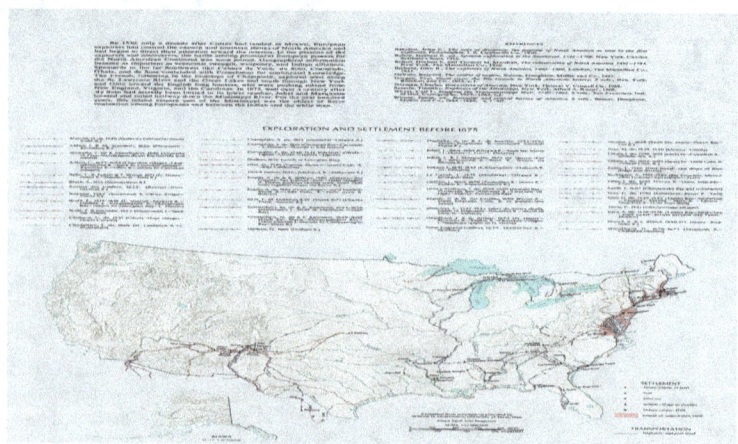

Exploration and Settlement prior to 1675

Chapter Two:
Florida's Missions: 1565-1700

From Martin Luther's edicts, the Reformation had gained momentum in Europe and by 1564; the French Huguenots had settled and claimed territory on the North Atlantic coast of Florida. Spain's reaction and actions were swift and brutal. In a town 14 miles south of what became Saint Augustine, Matanzas, (Place of Slaughters), the soldiers put to death every Huguenot. Fortifications against the enemy were necessary and a year later on 28 August, 1565, the Feast day of Augustine of Hippo, Father Francisco Lopez de Mendoza celebrated the first Mass, singing the traditional Te Deum hymn. Saint Augustine is considered where the first Roman Catholic mass was given on the first permanent European settlement of the United States. Except for twenty of the next two hundred years, St. Augustine was under Spanish rule and earned the nickname, 'la siempre fiel ciudad', 'the ever faithful city', and was administrated through the Diocese of Santiago in

Cuba. Saint Augustine's first mission church was named by Father Mendoza, Nombre de Dios, Name of God. The difficulty was navigating the rest of Florida and north through Georgia and South Carolina for settlements and Catholic mission work as the climate posed almost a formidable enemy. The Natives were nomadic tribes and therefore more challenging to keep in one place long enough for teaching the catechism. Father Mendoza gave complete reign to his missionaries to go forth and teach all the precepts of the Catholic Church.

The decades following began the 'golden age' for the Church in the Americas and fortified by the newly ordained Order of Saint Ignatius' Jesuits. Many gains were achieved, but more often in the early days, tragedy outweighed the triumphs. They had arrived in 1566 by the Jesuit General, Saint Francis Borgia, but due to setbacks, by 1572 the Jesuits left Florida to the Spanish Franciscans.

The Franciscans arrived in St. Augustine in 1577. Redoubling their efforts, they gained greater success until the Guale Uprising in 1597, when several missionaries were killed indiscriminately. In the twenty years prior, a mission chain was set up from Saint Augustine to the hills of Tallahassee. By 1655, there were 70 missions and 26,000 Catholic converts of Native Americans. The gains throughout the 17th century were enormous, but by the beginning of the 18th century, the enemy was in the guise of English colonists and they proved far more equipped to deal with the spreading of 'papist problem' – they held the sanctions from King George himself. By 1763, there were only four missions on the peninsula serving the 136 Catholic Native Americans. John Glimary Shea, the nineteen-century historian, called the campaign a form of religious cleansing and the extermination of the Apalachee missions "a mark of English provincial hatred against the Church of God." In 1763, the Spanish crown lost Havana during the Seven Year's War, (1756-1763: known as Queen Anne's War in the colonies) and Catholicism was all but wiped out in Florida.[5]

QUESTIONS

1. Knowing the Commandments – how would you as a Spanish soldier conducted yourself after the battle against the French Huguenots on the North Coast of Florida when they had been captured and the orders were given for them to be put to death?
2. Surrounded in the wilds of Northern Florida building a mission with the likelihood of being attacked – how well would you be able to keep your faith?
3. The reports of missionary deaths are returning to Spain, would you be able to submit to your vow of obedience?
4. Write a diary of your voyage and first year of travelling beyond Saint Augustine.

---

5   Catholicism in Florida By Dr. Charles Gallagher, SJ

The Georgia Martyrs

In 1587, five friars arrived in Spanish Florida, Fray Pedro de Corpa, Blas de Rodriguez, Fray Miguel de Anon and Francisco de Verascola. They were sent to the Guale village of Tolomato, the Spanish had it named Nuestra Senora de Guadalupe Tolomato Our Lady of Guadalupe of Tolomato.

The Guale Uprising

For the next decade, all things on reflection, the years passed peaceably enough until a young native man, though baptized and vowed himself to follow the Catholic faith, broke away in anger and defiance. Juanillo was to succeed his father as the Guale chief. The trouble erupting when went he went back to his cultural heritage and took on a second wife, thus committing a mortal sin, yet in his eyes, he was returning to his tribal ways. Father Corpa remonstrated and admonished that a Catholic cleaves to only one wife. Juanillo took little heed. To understand our own inclinations towards defiance and disobedience, it may serve as an example to render the following scene by imagination. Perhaps the dressing down was public one and his fellow tribesmen witnessed the rebuke. Though content in their faith, they were perchance torn in their allegiance, yet adhering to their promise, also called Juanillo to account. Father Corpa sought counsel from Father Blas de Rodriguez, the Spanish superior of all the Guale missions and as a consequence to his mortal sin, deprived Juanillo of his right to succeed his father as Chief.

From all reports, Father Corpa was known as a kindly and generous friar to all contrite sinners, but Juanillo, refused and in revenge of the humiliation of a monk's decree, struck back with a calculated vengeance; murder of the Franciscans. Enlisting others weary of the mission's yoke, he systematically planned and instigated the death of only the friars of each mission.

Martyrdom of Fray Pedro de Corpa

On 14 September, the feast day of the Exaltation of the Holy Cross, Fr. Corpa prepared the morning mass. Juanillo and his men came prepared as a war party. They rushed the priest and killed him with their stone hatchets. Afterwards they severed Fr. Corpa's head and impaled it on a stick by the river amid their own celebrations. Father Corpa's body stayed exposed for several days before being buried in an unmarked grave in the woods.

Martyrdom of Fray Blas de Rodríguez

Juanillo sent word to the *Guale* chief on St. Catherine's Island, kill the missionaries there. He remained on the mainland gathering more warriors and moved north to the village of Tupiqui, where Fr. Blas de Rodríguez lived. Juanillo surrounded him and relayed that his death was at hand and kept the friar hostage for two days. On 16 September, they allowed him his last Mass, his homily containing only this;

> *'My sons, for me it is not difficult to die. Even if you do not cause it, the death of this body is inevitable. We must be ready at all times, for we, all of us, have to die someday. But what does pain me is that the Evil One has persuaded you to do this offensive thing against your God and Creator. It is a further source of deep grief to me that you are unmindful of what we missionaries have done for you in teaching you the way to eternal life and happiness.'*

After Mass Fr. Rodríguez distributed his belongings to the faithful and gave them instructions to always obey God's law. He was then bound and forced to watch on as the Indians desecrated his chapel. Shortly afterwards, Father Rodriguez was clubbed to death and his body left in the woods for several days until a *Guale* Christian buried him. Spanish soldiers later recovered Father Rodriguez's remains.

Martyrdom of Fray Miguel de Añon and Fray Antonio de Bádajoz

There were two missionaries on St. Catherine's Island, Fr. Miguel de Añon, a Spanish noble and his assistant and interpreter Br. Antonio de Bádajoz. News of Juanillo's revenge reached Fr. Anon and Br. Badajoz and rather than seeking escape, they offered a Mass. Fr. Añon gave Br. Bádajoz communion, and then they were killed, on 17 September – the anniversary when St. Francis received his Stigmata. Their mutilated bodies were buried by Christian Indians at the base of the large wooden cross Fr. Añon had erected.

Martyrdom of Fray Francisco de Veráscola

Juanillo proceeded south to kill Fr. Francisco de Veráscola as he was returning in a canoe from St. Augustine with supplies. Two of the Indians, feigned friendship while the rest killed him and buried his body. Father's Franciscan hood and sombrero were later recovered, but his body was never found.

Passion of Fray Francisco de Avila

When the Indians broke into his hut, Father Avila attempted to escape, but he was shot with three arrows and easily captured. Forced to walk a long distance to another Indian village, tortured and condemned to die. They abruptly changed their minds, deciding instead to keep the friar as a slave. For nine months, Fr. Avila was mistreated in captivity and to spite and test the priest's faith, the Indians tried to force him take a wife and other acts against his vows. Later he was sent to St. Augustine, where he recovered his health. The lone survivor of the *Guale* massacres, Father Avila invoked clerical immunity when the Spanish governor asked him to testify. The good friar feared that his words would be grounds to execute his abductors, and he was unwilling to incriminate them. Years later, after Fr. Avila went to Havana he wrote of his ordeal, and even then only under obedience to his superior.

Guale Uprising Aftermath

Following the death of the Franciscans, their Guale missions were disbanded, though seven years later, they were completely restored and although Spanish rule had been shaken and its forces depleted, the missions prospered for nearly a century. English colonists destroyed the missions in 1702 looking southward from South Carolina to expand commercial and land interests. The Treaty of the Pyrenees, which concluded the Thirty Years War, Spain, conceded, leaving France as the dominance of Europe. In the colonies, Spain's preeminence was eroding by the settlements of Virginia moving northward and of Stuart Charles II rewarding his adherents' grants in the Carolinas.

The presence of Spanish Catholics in North Florida was an affront to Colonel James Moore and his band of Carolina soldiers. They attacked Florida in 1702 and destroyed the city of St. Augustine, in the words of one historian, amid "burning, plunder, carnage, and enslavement." While Moore was unable to capture the ever-durable fortress Castillo de San Marco at St. Augustine, he torched the Franciscan Church, the friary and the library and within two years, he embarked on a campaign to eradicate all the Franciscan missions of Florida. It was said even Protestant writers of the time deplored the destruction, even with their hatred of Spain and the Church, for the library contained many precious works of the Fathers, even the Latin Bible was unable to be saved from the flames. Moore's operation was successful to the point that by 1763 there were only four missions left on the peninsula, serving 136 Catholic Native Americans. In the 19th century, Catholic historian John Glimary Shea called Moore's campaign a form of religious cleansing and his extermination of the Apalachee missions "a mark of English provincial hatred against the church of God. In 1763, the Spanish crown lost Havana, Cuba during the Seven Year's War (1756-1763); also known as Queen Anne's War. In the American Colonies, Catholicism lost its great footing on the Florida peninsula.

What is necessary to realize is the interwoven events in Europe, especially Catholic Europe, always has a direct bearing and impact on the governing of lives and subsequent results in the Americas. The great upheavals during the 16th and 17th centuries, the Reformation and the Counter Reformation carried its force, consequences and decisions, setting all missionaries and Catholics in oftimes in untenable and resistance situations.

On a side note, in 1612 the superior of the custody of Saint Helen (*Santa Elena*) reported to the Spanish king:

> *'Although the Indians did not martyr the friars for the faith (that is, because of any doctrine or article of faith which they preached), it is certain that they martyred them because of the law of God which the religious taught them. This is the reason the Indians themselves gave and still attest to.'*

The Cause for the Georgia Martyrs

The formal process to declare the five men to be "saints" took a significant step forward on April 16 of 2007r. At that time, the Church's special tribunal for the cause received and accepted the sworn testimony of the members of an historical commission, who have been studying the case since 1982. The next step in the process is the meeting of the tribunal with modern-day witnesses. This is an effort to ascertain whether the reputation for martyrdom continues to the present day.

Fr. Conrad Harkins, O.F.M., the Vice Postulator for the Cause of the Georgia Martyrs, thinks it is fitting that the Cause is being advanced today.

"I think the time for recognizing the Georgia Martyrs has come," he observed. "It would be wonderful if Hispanic Americans had Hispanic-American saint-heroes. French missionaries from Quebec have long been recognized. Hispanic Americans can rightly be inspired by the courage of these missionaries who first brought the Gospel to America and were willing to die for it.

If raised to the altar, these Spanish missionaries would join the six 17th-century Jesuit priests and the two lay companions

QUESTIONS

1. Knowing of the faith and the tenets required, why did Juanillo refuse the sacrament of confession?
2. Can you explain why he and his actions are not very different from present day Catholics?
3. Why do we disobey?

4. Would you be able to act as Father Avila did in refusing to testify against his captors?
5. Give reasons why these Friars should be canalized.

Chronological History of Religious Influence in the New World and Europe (1492-1598)

* 1492: _Christopher Columbus_ discovers the New World.
* 1493: With the _Inter caetera_, _Pope Alexander VI_ awards sole _colonial_ rights over most of the New World to Spain.
* January 22, 1506: Kaspar von Silenen and first contingent of Swiss mercenaries enter the Vatican during the reign of Pope Julius II. Traditional date of founding of the _Swiss Guards_.
* April 18, 1506: _Pope Julius II_ lays cornerstone of New Basilica of St. Peter.
* 1508: _Michelangelo_ starts painting the _Sistine Chapel ceiling_.
* October 31, 1517: _Martin Luther_ posts his _95 Theses_, protesting the sale of _indulgences_.
* 1516: Saint Sir _Thomas More_ publishes "_Utopia_" in Latin.
* 1519: _Spanish conquest of Mexico_ by _Hernando Cortes_.
* January 3, 1521: _Martin Luther_ finally excommunicated by _Pope Leo X_ in the bull _Decet Romanum Pontificem_.
* 1521: Baptism of the first Catholics in the Philippines, the first Christian nation in Southeast Asia. This event is commemorated with the feast of the _Sto. Niño_.
* October 17, 1521: Pope Leo X confers the title _Fidei Defensor_ to _Tudor King Henry VIII of England_ for his defense of the seven sacraments and the supremacy of the pope in _Assertio_

Septem Sacramentorum against *Protestantism*.
* May 6, 1527: *Sack of Rome*.
* 1531: *Our Lady of Guadalupe* appears to *Juan Diego* in *Mexico*.
* November 16, 1532: *Francisco Pizzaro* captures *Atahualpa*. Conquest of *Incan Empire*.
* August 15, 1534: *Saint Ignatius of Loyola* and six others, including *Francis Xavier* met in *Montmartre*, then just outside Paris, to found the missionary *Jesuit Order*.
* October 30, 1534: *English Parliament* passes *Act of Supremacy* making the King of England *Supreme Head of the Church of England*. *Anglican* schism with Rome.
* 1535: *Michelangelo* starts painting the *Last Judgement* in the *Sistine Chapel*.
* 1536 To 1540: *Dissolution of the Monasteries* in England, Wales and Ireland.
* December 17, 1538: *Pope Paul III* excommunicates *King Henry VIII* of England.
* 1540: *Pope Paul III* confirmed the order of the *Society of Jesus*.
* July 21, 1542: *Pope Paul III*, with the Constitution *Licet ab initio*, established the *Supreme Sacred Congregation of the Roman and Universal Inquisition*.
* 1543: A full account of the heliocentric *Copernican* theory titled, On the Revolutions of the Heavenly Spheres (De Revolutionibus Orbium Coelestium) is published. Considered as the start of the Scientific Revolution.
* December 13, 1545: Ecumenical *Council of Trent* convened during the pontificate of Paul III, to prepare the Catholic response to the *Protestant Reformation*. Its rulings set the tone of Catholic society for at least three centuries.

* December 4, 1563: Ecumenical _Council of Trent_ closed. The decrees were confirmed on January 26, 1564, by Pius IV in the Bull "Benedictus Deus".
* 1568: _St. John Chrysostom_, _St. Basil_, _St. Gregory Nazianzus_, _St. Athanasius_ and _St. Thomas Aquinas_ are made _Doctors of the Church_.
* July 14, 1570: Pope St. Pius V issues the Apostolic Constitution on the _Tridentine Mass_, Quo Primum.
* October 7, 1571: Christian fleet of the Holy League defeats the Ottoman Turks in the _Battle of Lepanto_.
* 1577: _Teresa of Avila_ writes _The Interior Castle_, one of the classic works of Catholic _mysticism_.
* February 24, 1582: Pope Gregory XIII issues the Bull _Inter gravissimas_ reforming the _Julian Calendar_.
* October 4, 1582: The _Gregorian Calendar_ is first adopted by Italy, Spain, and Portugal. October 4 is followed by October 15 – ten days are removed.
* September 28, 1586: Domenico Fontana successfully finished re-erecting the Vatican Obelisk at its present site in St. Peter's Square. Hailed as a great technical achievement of its time.
* 1593: _Robert Bellarmine_ finishes his _Disputationes de controversiis christianae fidei_.
* 1598: Papal role in _Peace of Vervins_.

Chapter Three:
The Faith from the North: French Territories, Missionaries The Jesuit Martyrs

Ad Majorem Dei Gloriam!

October 19 commemorates the martyrdom of six priests of the Society of Jesus and their two lay companions who worked with them tirelessly.

Jesuit Priests:

* St. Jean de Brébeuf
* St. Noel Chabanel

* **St. Anthony Daniel**
* **St. Charles Garnier**
* **St. Issac Joques**
* **St. Gabriel Lalemant**

Laymen:

* **St. Rene Goupil** – (surgeon and lay apostle, first to be martyred, Sept 29. 1642)
* **St. Jean de la Lande**

France of the early seventeenth century provided a direct impact and great influence on the North American continent. The fruits of the Counter Reformation created a rejuvenated and revived religious commitment, remarkable in her lasting accomplishments in France and in the mission fields. Within these was also the revitalization of exploration coupled with the renewed vigor of spreading Catholicism farther afield. An appeal was made by Francis I of France to concentrate their efforts along what is now the states bordering Canada and Canada herself. He knew and conceded that the right of sovereignty and colonization depended on the sanction of the Pope. Francis petitioned Pope Clement VII to reverse the Inter caetera for those lands unoccupied and unexplored by the Spaniards. It was granted and 1534, (the same year by the by England's Parliament passed the Act of Supremacy making the King of England Supreme Head of the Church of England. The Anglican schism with Rome) saw the French expedition journey across North America.

The one who comes most readily to mind is of course, Champlain who began by the founding of Quebec in 1608. Her original course was a trading post and center and for the housing of priests and in 1615 at his request, the Recollects arrived for the continuity of faith for the traders, but also for the spread of the Catholic faith to the native tribes. Champlain had already established friendly relationships with the Algonquins, who were nomadic and the Hurons, who were more settled of the tribes. Yet there was a formable enemy, the war culture of the Iroquois – who gained much in the way of processions with their constant attacks upon the more peaceful and trading tribes. To prevent or rather to stem the advance of further trouble for his own explorations along the Saint Lawrence, and to give safety for his trading allies, Champlain dispatched troops for the sole purpose of defeating the Iroquois and ensure their forces stayed scattered. The French force succeeded, yet left the Iroquois with a lasting and deep hatred for the French regardless whether they be secular or religious. Yet there was also a far more dangerous enemy, which encompassed both the warring tribes and France's allied tribes; the subtle superstitions against what the Europeans carried with them; disease, which none on these shores had ever encountered. Smallpox is now considered unheard of and measles and the flu, an innocuous childhood passage, but for the Native Americans, these three were deadly and its introduction almost decimated many of the clans. In consequence, any of the converts who were somewhat shaky with the Catholic faith, their witchdoctors gained greater control and almost succeeded in battling away the Jesuit influence. However, the distinctive fervor of the Jesuits and their approach was rooted in a disciplined common sense that contained itself in the willingness to stay and live among the Native Americans first before their advancing the necessity of conversion. They were aware of the valid differences in the cultures from theirs and reasoned the teaching of the catechism would be far acceptable to attain at the least by learning and knowing the native language and their way of life. In many ways, the burden was on the priests for the language of the various tribes of the natives. For their dialects were varied, yet it was and is an oral tradition of sounds and infections representing the diverse use of speech. The sense of the written word of itself was a complex and foreign idiom, which could hardly contain the vast and varied meanings of their own tongue. The reality was a painstaking translation of the Latin texts to convey the wonder of the scriptures, though which they found the use of the Gregorian Chant far easier to convey, for its intonations of rhythm and sound matched more readily with the speech patterns of the First Americans.

From the spiritual diaries by Saint John de Brébeuf, priest and martyr, conveys most aptly the commitment the Jesuits brought to the New World:

> *For two days now I have experienced a great desire to martyr and to endure all the torments the martyrs suffered.*
>
> *Jesus, my Lord and Savior, what can I give you in return for all the favors you have first conferred on me? I will take from your hand the cup of your sufferings and call on your Name. I vow before your eternal Father and the Holy Spirit, before your most holy Mother and her chaste spouse, before the angels, apostles and martyrs, before my blessed fathers Saint Ignatius and Saint Xavierin truth I vow to you, Jesus my Savior, that as far as I have the strength I will never fail to accept the grace of martyrdom, if some day you in your infinite mercy you should offer it to me, your most unworthy servant.*
>
> *I bind myself in this way so that for the rest of my life I will have neither permission nor freedom to refuse opportunities of dying and shedding my blood for you, unless at a particular juncture I should consider it more suitable for your glory to act otherwise at that time. Further, I*

bind myself to this so that, on receiving the blow of death, I shall accept it from your hands with the fullest and joy of spirit. For this reason, my beloved Jesus and because of the surging joy which moves me, now I offer my blood and body and life. May I die only for you, if you will grant me this grace, since you willingly died for me. Let me so live that you may grant me the gift of such a happy death. In this way my God and Savior, I will take from your hand the cup of sufferings and call on your Name: Jesus, Jesus, Jesus.

My God, it grieves me greatly that you are not known, that in this savage wilderness all have not been converted to you, that sin has not been driven from it. My God, even if all the brutal tortures which prisoners in this region must endure should fall on me; I offer myself most willingly to them and I alone shall suffer them all.

By 1625, the Recollects were in sore need of reinforcements and the arrival of the first of many Jesuits, of whom, Father Brébeuf was the first, knowing full well of the fate in Guale and all martyrs before them, willing to accepted the same and gave themselves as our first martyrs. The good Fathers Brébeuf, Chabanel, Daniel, Garnier, Joques, Lalemant, and their companion laymen, Goupil and Lande. These are the saints over the course of the next fourteen years, who gave their relief and aid to the Recollects who needed to further expand their missionary efforts, they had just extended as far as the Huron nation, 800 miles west of Quebec. It was In Huronia, where the first Jesuit missionaries took up their post, visiting the scattered Indian villages, and at the time, well received by several of the Indian families in their own dwellings.

The next fourteen years proved peaceful enough and the priests' missionary efforts to the Hurons gained much in the way of conversion to the true faith. With the addition of more missionaries from France, by necessity, the decision to construct a Christian settlement was realized by 1639 and so began Sainte Marie. The original building, built in the Huron style of a single bark covered cabin, housed ten Jesuits and five workmen. The construction continued and soon Sainte Marie grew to be a fortified village with a residence for 27 priests and 39 French laborers, a church, storehouses for food and equipment, a hospital, and living quarters for visiting Indians. Now with a solid base, the mission was able to prepare hundreds of Indians for baptism and began constructing churches throughout the Huron villages.

In the arduous years since 1625, 1649 bore the brunt and disregarding the success, turned its face and grimaced on the ferocity of torture meted out specifically to the Blackrobes. Though the difficulties arrived far earlier. In the later part of 1636 when Fathers Charles Garnier and Isaac Jogues joined Father Brébeuf, through 1637, influenza reared itself into an epidemic, not only in the winter, but reasserted itself once again in the autumn. Father Jogues fell victim and came close to dying, the French, their immunity compromised suffered and the majority of the Hurons, without the benefit of resistance, succumbed. Father Jogues recovered after several weeks and none of the French perished, but the many Hurons who survived, grew resentful and suspicious, incited by their sorcerers. The belief they aroused was the only reason the Blackrobes did not die was from their own sorcery and adding to the fears, they brought the pestilence so that the French could take all the Huron land after the disease obliterated them all. In the early months of 1637, the disease receded and diminished as did the haranguing and distrust from the Hurons.

The key events that eased the malingering wariness were the baptisms of two prominent Huron chiefs, Tsiouendaentaha, who came from the nation of Ihonataria and Chihwatenhwa from Ossossane. As they did not dropped dead immediately as the natives were certain they would, many began to doubt their sorcerers' accusations. Now called Peter and Joseph respectively, these men became an edification to the missionaries and a source of wonderment to their fellow Hurons.

But the inroads gained were short-lived and by early autumn the influenza was again rampant among the Hurons and this time those who suspected the cause to be the Jesuits, exhibited blatant hostility towards them. Father Brébeuf bade his companions to be ready for death at any moment and ordered a novena of Masses to begin in honor of Saint Joseph. He composed a letter to which was sent to his Superior at Quebec. Dated October 28, 1637, it reads in part:

> *"We are perhaps upon the point of shedding our blood and of sacrificing our lives in the service of our good Master, Jesus Christ. It seem that His Goodness is willing to accept this sacrifice from me for the expiation of my great innumerable sins, and to crown from this hour forward the past services and the great and ardent desires of all our priests who are here....But we are all grieved over this, that these barbarians, through their own malice, are closing the door to the Gospel and to Grace.... Whatever conclusion they reach, and whatever treatment they accord us, we will try, by the Grace of Our Lord, to endure it patiently for His service. It is a singular favor that His Goodness gives us, to allow us to endure something for love of Him...."*

On that same day, following the Indian tradition of feasting prior to one's death, Father Brébeuf invited the all to his death banquet. Their residence was filled to capacity by a mob of hungry Hurons, who glutted themselves with sagamite' while Father Brébeuf chanted his death song in the Huron tongue. With precise imagery, he depicted the eternal joys of the blessed in heaven and with a greater vividness, the torments of the damned in hell. Those listening were enthralled, this was a death chant they had never heard before. In addition, from the good Father's eloquence and passion, the Indians, departing from the feast well filled, yet with troubled minds, their condemnation of the Blackrobes wavered in their pronouncement.

Aware of the certainty that any display of fear on their part would be reasoned as a sign of guilt, they went about their duties in the village seemingly oblivious to the serious dangers existing. Throughout their days, the good Fathers were not molested nor threatened, in fact, when the novena to Saint Joseph was completed a week later, a tranquility pervaded Huronia, which even the Indians, could not help but notice. The Blackrobes marveled at God's protection and the powerful intercession of their faithful guardian, Saint Joseph.

The epidemic did subside a few months later and cases of persecution, become rare. The occasion of such incidents was usually the act of angered sorcerers rather than the dangerous mobs they incited. Intrigued by the mysteries of the Catholic Faith, some of the Huron chiefs began to invite the priests to their councils for the sole purpose of discussing religion. Thankful to advance the message of salvation, the good Fathers held special feasts wherein they preached to all those gathered. Though many came out of curiosity, a small but distinguished group, including the chiefs and elders, became increasingly interested in what the missionaries were speaking of and from this, a few of the Hurons at Ossossane' were requesting private instructions in the Faith, and the number of adult baptisms began to increase.

Ossossane was one of the extensive and numerous Huron settlements and, encouraged by the reaching out and holding onto the faith, Father Brébeuf was encouraged to extend the missions to include all of the Huron Nation. To gain leave to travel as a simple missionary, his petitioned for relief of being the superior of the settlement was granted and in August of 1639, Father Jerome Lalemant was appointed to succeed him. (He was the uncle to the future martyr Gabriel Lalemant who joined the mission as a Donne in 1648) Under his direction, Sainte Marie was proclaimed a permanent site as the Jesuit mission base to central on its own for the widespread Huron village. From her an organized system of records could be more easily contained and sent to Europe to keep all informed of the good works the Fathers. This was a common and necessary requirement for all Jesuit missionaries. The accounts are known as the Jesuit Relations and as such were published to engender interest and enthusiasm for their missionary work alongside with their parish logs, which were kept at the mission.

To give greater clarity of the number of converts and to include the decimation that occurred between disease and the constant war parties of the Iroquois, consensuses were taken every few years. The one for 1639 was a drastic one, the number of Hurons in the thirty-two surrounding villages, numbered twenty thousand, whereas four years earlier there were thirty thousand, and now the human toll was about to decline again by the hundreds, in September the epidemic of smallpox arrived in force. For the Fathers, once again were suspected, threatened and expelled from every village they went to care for, giving Father Jerome to write, "We have sometimes wondered whether we could hope for the conversion of this country without the shedding of blood.... For in the words of the ancient axiom, "The blood of martyrs is the seed of the Church."

Martyrdom of Rene' Goupil

Within three years, the Huron Mission became destitute, due to the rain and a poor harvest, food was scarce and there was little in the way of medicine, clothing, especially vestments and the needs for the altar. By necessity, an arduous expedition began for Quebec for the much needed supplies. Father Jogues lead the company of five Frenchmen and eighteen Hurons. The journey there and back would cover approximately nineteen hundred miles total and evade the warring parties of the Iroquois all along the Saint Lawrence River. They left in June and arrived a month later in Quebec, safe for the time being. With the addition of thirty-five Hurons and the Christian Chief Ahatsistari, who lead the party, the Donne', Rene Goupil (his talents being desirous in Sainte Marie, he was an excellent nurse and a skilled surgeon) joined Father Jogues along with several French workmen. The second day after their departure proved fatal, the Iroquois attacked and those not killed were taken captive to endure the traditional 'welcoming party' for prisoners of war when the Iroquois returned to their village. Known as 'running the gauntlet', amidst heart shattering screams of victory, captives were forced to run up a hill one at a time between parallel columns of Indians welding clubs and thorned rods, their blood lust easily contagious to one another. Considered a special guest, Father Jogues was the last to run, the frenzy meting out the worst of the blows. Stumbling and stunned, they dragged the rest of the way to the top of the hill. Gaining conscious, Father Jogues suffered through the burning of his arms and legs with a torch and one ripping off his thumb with their teeth.

The endurance of faith had yet to begin, for Father Jogues and his fellow twenty prisoners. Death was not to be the easy escape; the Iroquois required them to be marched some days for the viewing of their whole nation, such prizes of war necessitated the showing. Marched and paraded through the villages of Ossernenon

(Auriesville, New York), Andagaron (Randall, New York) and finally to Tionontoguen (Sprakers, New York). In all the same length of torture continued unabated, most especially for Father Jogues. By his being a Blackrobe, the Dutch, with vigor warned the villages of the French priests, for they were sorcerers and most particularly the Protestants, cautioned, beware of the sign they used with their right hand, a movement resembling the sign of the cross. In consequence, the Indians vied for the 'privilege' of crunching Father Jogues' fingers in their mouths and in further tempting of abandoning faith, in Ossernenon, an Algonquin woman, baptized into the faith, was forced to saw off Father Jogues' left thumb with an oyster shell.

The tribal chiefs, gathering in Tionontoguen held council to decide the prisoners' fate. The Hurons, given torture and death, the white men spared for the fetching of ransom, knowing the reverence the French felt for their priests.

Required to witness, Father Jogues in bitter agony watched the slaughter of his children. He later wrote; "While each one suffered his own pain, I suffered that of all. I was afflicted with a great anguish, great as one may believe the heart of a most loving parent is afflicted when he sees the suffering of his own children." He also heard the reports of Ahatsistari's death sentence in another village and from those who were there, they gave authority to his prayers aloud for his persecutors.

Left to heal for bargaining, Father Jogues and Rene' Goupil were free to move about the village and visit the longhouses, though the instructions were to avoid any action that would irritate and cause their captors to rescind their generosity. Yet, though Father Jogues well experienced in forbearance, Goupil was still young and caught making the sign the cross over an ill child. Retribution came swift and on 29 September, 1642, the feast day of Saint Michael the Archangel, Rene' Goupil became the first American martyr. It was not until the spring when Father Jogues found his fractured skull and the remains of his bones. He buried him beneath the trunk of a tree.

Martyrdom of Father Issac Jogues

For thirteen months, during which Father Jogues, though forced from village to village by his tenuous title of 'bargaining chip' among the Iroquois and Mohawk tribes, labored in quiet, his covert operation for converts gained seventy of the enemy prior to their deaths. Though extorted to escape by the Dutch who settled Albany, Father Jogues stayed on preaching the Catholic faith until news reached him of another defeat of the Iroquois by the French. The sentence of death was passed on him and with prayer, he realized escape was part of God's plan and on Christmas Day in 1643, Father Jogues was back in France. Overwhelmed by the attention and devotions of the people hearing of his ordeals, he begged leave to return to New France and back to his mission work. Given special permission by Pope Urban VIII to say Mass, despite his missing fingers, the Pontiff stated; 'It is unbefitting that a martyr of Christ should not drink the blood of Christ.' Knowing he would not return, Father Jogues stated on his departure; 'I go, but I shall never come back again.' He arrived back in Quebec in June of 1644. In October of 1646, Father Jogues along with the donne' John de Lalande were martyred, their heads placed on pikes and their bodies thrown in the river.

By 1647, the Hurons were gradually becoming a Catholic nation and would have expanded had it not been for the continual attacks from the Iroquois. Father Noel Chabanel had joined Father Brébeuf the year prior and found learning the languages and attempting to accustom himself to the Indians way of life somewhat repugnant. He kept these sentiments to himself however and vowed to remain and give his life as a missionary.

Martyrdom of Father Antony Daniel

Father Anthony Daniel prior to his ordination, studied for the law in Dieppe, France. Shortly after joining the Jesuits, he arrived in 1634, a year after Father Brébeuf had returned from France for the last time. He assisted Father Brébeuf in Huronia for several years, before being sent to the mission village of Saint Joseph renamed from the Indian, Teanaostaye. Both, by their years of service, were acknowledged as the oldest missionaries in the field.

It was in June of 1648 when Father Daniel came to Sainte Marie to visit with his old friend Father Brébeuf and for the retreat in the spiritual exercises of Saint Ignatius. Leaving in early July to return, it was Father Brébeuf's role to piece together from a handful of survivors, how in the attack on Saint Joseph's, Father Daniel was killed. Shortly after the morning Mass, a force of several hundred rushed into the village, slaying all in their path. Father Daniel, holding the crucifix before him walked towards the oncoming Iroquois so that the Hurons would have a chance to escape. The Iroquois, recognizing him fired muskets, a ball piercing Father Daniel's heart, the arrows they shot, pierced his face and neck. Setting the chapel on fire, they scalped him and then threw Father Daniel's body into the flames.

Martyrdom of Fathers Brébeuf and Lalemant

In January of 1649, Father Gabriel Lalemant, (the nephew of Jerome Lalemant, the former Superior of the Huron mission), arrived, having been appointed to become Father Brébeuf's assistant. His tenure was short, for on March 15th, 1649, the Iroquois once again attacked the mission and he and Father Brébeuf were taken prisoner. The course of treatment received did not differ from the fates of Rene' Goupil and Father Jogues except in the greater degree of ferocity and desecration. They were marched to Saint Ignace, which for Father Brébeuf's dream was to become the citadel for the whole mission. Once again, the parallel lines and they were beaten through it and then dragged to a cabin Father Brébeuf envisioned one day as the Church in Saint Ignace.

With the five other prisoners, Father Brébeuf and they were commanded to sing their death chant. For the good Father, he in the Huron language sang forth with hymns to the Savior. While he sang, the Iroquois chewed his fingers to shreds, and then led him to a post to which he kissed as if it were the Cross of Christ. He knew well the code of conduct under torture, if forced to cry out for mercy, the Indians indeed became the victors, but Father Brébeuf vowed to defy the code to the end and not utter one plea for mercy.

With systematic sadism, burning sticks were placed underneath the priest's feet then burning torches applied to his legs. One warrior pushed a firebrand around his neck and beneath his armpits and still no word from Father Brébeuf. They then sliced off pieces of his flesh and the only words heard were not anguish, but only "Jesus, taiteur!" (Jesus, have mercy on us). To silence, they shoved flaming torches in his mouth and in a mockery of a halo, red-hot hatchets tied together were dropped on his head. The addition of a belt of burning bark was strapped around his waist so that Father Brébeuf became enveloped in smoke from his roasting skin. He only prayed aloud for the souls of his persecutors. There was one, a former Christian Huron who betrayed his people and his faith spoke back, "You say that Baptism and the sufferings of this life head straight to Paradise; you will soon go, for I am going to baptize you and make you suffer well, in order to go sooner to your paradise." He then took a pot full of boiling water and poured it over Father Brébeuf's head saying; "Go to heaven, for you are well baptized." Father Brébeuf responded again with "Jesus taiteur." At this point, the evil done went further, they chopped of his nose, lips and his tongue and another flaming torch was shoved against his face. Father Brébeuf's last words; "Jesus, taiteur." The final infliction was to burn shut the priest's still open eyes.

Father Lalemant received the same with an added measure when he was heard praying to God. They cut out his tongue and thrust fiery faggots in his mouth, then plucked out his eyes and shoved in burning coals. His hands were subsequently sliced off and seared with red-hot axes. Father Lalemant responded in the same, "Jesus, taiteur."

When their blackened and mutilated corpses were recovered from Saint Ignace, they were carried back to Sainte Marie, vested in sacerdotal garments, and laid out side by side all night before the Blessed Sacrament. On Sunday March 21st, 1649, they were buried by Father Ragueneau with the words; "…that I know none who did not desire, rather than fear a similar death."

Later he read Father Brébeuf's spiritual diary and came across these words; "Two days in succession, I have felt in me a great desire for martyrdom and for enduring all the torments which the martyrs have suffered." Father Ragueneau recalled a conversation with the good priest several years prior. He had asked if he would be afraid of the fire should the Iroquois ever capture him. Father Brébeuf had replied; "Oh yes, I would fear it if I regarded only my own weakness. The sting of the fly is capable of making me impatient. But I trust that God will help me. Aided by his grace, I do not fear the torments of the fire any more than I fear the prick of a pin."

Martyrdom of Fathers Garnier and Chabanel

In the southwest among the Petuns were four Jesuit priests. In the village Etarita, Father Garnier, who had labored there for ten years, and Father Chabanel who was stationed with him. In another village, twelve miles north, resided Fathers Grelon and Garreau. Unwilling to risk the lives of any more priests, Father Ragueneau sent a letter commanding all four priests to return to Saint Joseph's at once unless there was an urgent need to stay. Father Garnier ordered Father Chabanel to leave with the Huron refugees.

On 7 December, 1649, two days after Father Chabanel's departure, the dreaded sound of Iroquois sped through the village. Father Garnier ran to the chapel, extorting all to escape any way you can and to keep your faith. Those surrounding him pleaded for him to make his escape with them, but he only returned to face the invaders. Muskets were fired at him and he was shot in the breast and in the stomach. Father Garnier attempted to give absolution to the dying around him, but a tomahawk ended his movements.

For Father Chabanel, he was struggling through the woods trying to keep pace with his companions. Finally he told them to go on without him. They feared for his life if they left him behind, but he insisted they go ahead. "It makes no difference if I die, the Iroquois cannot rob me of the blessedness of paradise." A lone Huron doubled back and came upon the unsuspecting priest by a stream. He was heard to boast later; "I rid the world of a carrion of a Frenchman, brained him at his own feet, and threw his body in the river." The day was 8 December, 1649, the Feast of the Immaculate Conception of the Blessed Virgin Mary. In the spring of 1650, Sainte Marie was abandoned and the Jesuits with what remained of their haggard flock, returned to Quebec.[67]

Considered perhaps a failed mission after so many years, the labors of the martyrs were not left bereft, for the souls of many were saved and the seeds of faith planted with their own blood. Their successors were there to reap the fruit, ironically in the person of the Blessed Kateri Tekakwitha, the Lily of the Mohawks.

The Eight North American Martyrs and their birthdates into eternity:

* **Saint Rene' Goupil — September 29, 1642**
* **Saint Isaac Jogues — October 18, 1646**
* **Saint John de Lalande — October 19, 1646**
* **Saint Anthony Daniel — July 4, 1648**
* **Saint John de Brébeuf — March 16, 1649**
* **Saint Gabriel Lalemant — March 17, 1649**
* **Saint Charles Garnier — December 7, 1649**
* **Saint Noel Chabanel — December 8, 1649**[8]

Prayer to the Eight North American Martyrs (author unknown)

---

6 **Jesuit North American Martyrs -www.wf-f.org/Jesuit_Martyrs.html**
7 The Eight North American Martyrs_catholicism.org/eight-na-**martyrs**.html
8 Fromm, Joseph http://goodjesuitbadjesuit.blogspot.jesuithistory

Let Us Pray

Protect our land, O heavenly patrons, which you have bedewed with the rich treasure of your blood. Watch over our Catholic Faith which you helped to establish in this new land. Bring all our fellow citizens to a knowledge and love of the truth. Make us zealous in spreading abroad a knowledge of Catholic teachings, so that we may continue and perfect the work which you have begun with so much labor and suffering. Pray for our homes, our schools, our missions; for vocations, for the conversion of sinners, the return of those who have wandered from the fold, and the perseverance of all the faithful. Amen.

The sacred "Ravine" at Auriesville. To be alone in this place where a martyr shed his blood for Christ is a sobering thing. The silence is great and the atmosphere enters into your very soul as one considers the sacrifices made to bring the truths of the Gospel to others in a strange land.

What need is there for missionaries if, as many today erroneously contend, the only requirement for salvation is personal sincerity in whatever one believes? Indeed, the very life of all apostolic labors is Our Lord's command to 'teach' every human creature the truths necessary for their salvation. Our Lord added to this commission, "He that believeth and is baptized, shall be saved: but he that believeth not shall be condemned."

The North American Martyrs were canonized by Pope Pius XI in 1930. Their feast day is celebrated on October 19th in the United States.

QUESTIONS

1. Would we be able to suffer as well as these martyrs did today? Bear in mind these tortures are not unknown in our modern time.
2. What gave these martyrs their great strength and fortitude in their faith?
3. Why did the Iroquois and Mohawk tribes despise and hate the Blackrobes with such intensity?
4. Why did the Huron tribes convert to the faith with more ease than other tribes?
5. As a Jesuit missionary, write your own spiritual diary for the year of 1649

Chapter Four:
Blessed Kateri Tekakwitha 1656-1680

In the village of Ossernenon, seven short years after the blood of the Jesuit martyrs still wept into the earth, Kateri Tekakwitha was born. Her mother, Kahenta, was an Algonquin convert, who had been captured by the Mohawks. The War Chief of the Turtle clan, Kenhoronkwa, who chose her for his wife, saved her from the ritual captive's fate. He married her in full Mohawk tradition and she bore him a daughter and a son.

Unable to practice her faith openly, Kahenta kept the memories alive of the slain martyrs by singing Christian hymns to her

---

9   www.catholicherald.org/archives/articles

10 http://gosw.about.com/od/santafenewmexico/ig

daughter, telling her the brave stories of the Jesuits and by teaching her how to pray. The time was short lived for small pox invaded the Mohawk settlement when Kateri was four and she lost her parents and her brother. She herself became quite ill and though nursed back to health, Kateri's eyesight was severely damaged as a result and her face scarred by the epidemic.

Adopted in her orphan state by her uncle Iowerano, the family left behind the death and rebuilt their lives near what is now Fonda, New York. As with many villages, the elder matrons guided the life in each tribal compound. The men were the warriors and hunters and had little say or involvement of domestic affairs. (On a side note, the elder women also decided the fate of captives and took part in the ritual torture and slaying of prisoners and elected the chiefs for the Five Nation Confederacy.) As such, they were the women who guarded the maiden Kateri because of her high ranking and her being an orphan. In their tradition, these individuals are given special attention and care. For Tekakwitha, also called Tegarouita, meaning 'she who advances or opens the way before her', for names mean a great deal in response to a valuable characteristic in Indian culture. For Kateri, the seeds her mother bestowed were beginning to flourish.

Despite the handicap of her eyesight, or perhaps because of it, Kateri, learning all aspects of daily duties, was found to be quite adept at the intricate sewing of designs for the ornamentation on the clothing. Each piece highly prized and Kateri was observed to be quite a willingly worker and sweet tempered. Though all this, marriage also was discussed by her aunts, but Kateri stayed reticent from such conversations. Her reaction, considered stemming from a modesty and shyness, the aunts resolved to be patient, feeling Kateri would adjust in time to the acceptable ways of life. Yet, unbeknownst to the elders, Kateri was embarking on a spiritual journey and glimpsing a vital dimension of the Catholic faith, an aspect well beyond her caretakers' existence.

In 1667, after a treaty with the French, a mission had opened in Caughnawaga. Three Jesuits priests, Fathers Fremin, Brutas and Pierron arrived to begin their missionary efforts among the Mohawks and though Iowerano was dubious about their visit, he invited his guests with welcoming ceremonies where Kateri attended and served. When questioned, the priests were impressed with her sweet docility.

True to Jesuit understating and responsiveness for incorporating and honoring the traditions of other cultures, Father John Pierron, the first pastor of the new mission, used his talents to design scenes and symbols to illustrate and teach the Mohawks the Catholic faith for our journey from life to death. His successor, Father Francis Boniface was a linguist and learning the Mohawk language, translated prayers and devotions for his flock. Shortly after a mission choir was formed and for those attending, the liturgical chant became far readily accessible for understanding. Though Kateri was not an active participant in the services, she watched, observed, and kept all in her heart, seeing the necessity of pray and meditation while going about her daily chores. To further enhance the validity of Christ the King for the lost and forsaken, Christmas in the chapel was celebrated the manager and the Babe who came to rescue all those in sore need of his protection. Still without formal training, Kateri began to see and experience His divine love and to seek ways to offer praise and thanksgiving.

At this most wondrous season in Caughnawaga, Father Boniface brought home thirty Mohawks and learned to trust another; Kryn, called the 'Great Mohawk' by all the clans. Residing in the Catholic enclave Sault Mission on the Saint Lawrence River, being a haven for converts, Kryn encouraged Father Boniface to move all converts there to live in peace as Christians. This exodus, beginning in the following December, alarmed Iowerano, his fear the new way of life would destroy the forging of the nations, which took centuries to build. Regardless of Iowerano's dismay at the loss of so many, Father Boniface returned to the mission, but not long after he passed away on the 17 December, 1674. His successor, Father Jacques de Lamberville became aware of Kateri's piety with his first conversation with her and her speaking of her Christian mother and her knowledge of the Catholic faith. On requesting baptism, Father Lamberville was somewhat taken aback. He was sentient of her place in the tribe, the daughter of one chief and the ward of another, there was the necessity to be prudent and take great care for her appeal, for though the missionaries were gaining success with the Mohawks, the tenuous relationship still could evoke considerable wrath. Father Lamberville urged patience and her need for attending the catechetical classes, which would lead to her baptism. Kateri agreed quite amiably and by her phrases and her radiance when discussing matters of the soul, Father Lamberville began to suspect that Kateri was spiritually mature beyond her nineteen years.

Though the elders did not oppose her attendance for catechism, feeling perhaps Kateri would be better off among those her own age; their irritation was directed to her continual refusals of marriage offers. The state was a normal course for a young maiden and in consequence, they punished her severely for her consistent stand against their decision. Through all Kateri submitted with grace and meekness to their treatment and they grudgingly respected her strength and resolve. There came from her uncle, not forbidding the classes regarding her conversion, for he knew of the unique unity of the Christian Mohawks, his concern and fears were that Kateri would forget her rank and obligations to her own clan in the flush of enthusiasm for her religious convictions. In actuality, Father Lamberville was more troubled than her uncle was. Granted, additional conversations proved she was a soul with many graces and gifts, yet such individuals can challenge and disconcert any missionary assigned to the North American territory. For Kateri was a child of the American wilderness not a cloistered nun or recluse studying scriptures and liturgies. Father Lamberville realized she was a mystically advanced soul who was clearly chosen by God to spiritual heights unknown by most humans and to a lifestyle few humans could understand, yet needing guidance, the good priest called on prayer and time to prove the stability and authenticity of Kateri's spiritual abilities. He intended to utilize the days and weeks of her catechetical schooling to investigate her life, and then he would be able to determine the depths of her soul and the will of God in her life.

Kateri attending all her classes and services in silence and serenity, while Father Lamberville inquired among the elders regarding her character, all reports agreed, Kateri was gentle, kindly, obedient and prudent in all her dealings with others. Outside the complaints for refusing marriage proposals, there was no scandal or gossip attached to her name, Father Lamberville recognized that Kateri was indeed a radiant vessel of grace, led by the Holy Spirit to union with God. So on Easter Sunday in 1676, Tekakwitha became Kateri, named after Saint Catherine of Sienna, the great mystic of Italy.

To start and stay on God's narrow path begets persecution and for Kateri hers began following her baptism. Keeping herself in meditation and pray, the practice brought the ire of family and companions and the complaint leveled against was she not only neglecting her duties, but also no longer taking part in the festivals and gatherings of the Mohawks. The term 'Christian' was directed at her with scorn and more menacing was from a young Mohawk warrior threatening to kill her if she did not promise to give up her Catholic faith and ways. The slander worsened when her aunt accused her of an improper relationship with her uncle. Alarmed, Father Lamberville spoke with her; Kateri did not complain and dismissed her humiliations and confrontations as insubstantial when compared to the sufferings of Christ. In private, he prayed for guidance to free Kateri from her tormentors. The gift came in the guise of a prominent Oneida chief; Garonhiague, a Strong Christian, who came to the settlement with two companions, one a relative of Kateri's on her mother's side. The decision was made to bring Kateri to the Saint Francis Xavier de Sault mission in the north. Entrusted to the Jesuits in 1667 by King Louis XIV of France, the site at Sault (French for rapids) was near La Prairie de Madeleine. The mission stood on a plateau by the Saint Lawrence River and some 120-150 Christian Indians who sought refuge resided there. The mission itself was surrounded by a stockade and the longhouses of the Indians were constructed outside so their own traditional ways of life could be practiced within the protection of the Catholic Church and within the framework of their own heritage. For the converts, the demand was not to assume the ways of the whites as part of their conversions, but instead encouraged to sanctify their own tribal customs in the way of Christ. Here Kateri had the given peace to deepen her faith.

On her arrival a letter addressed to the resident missionaries from Father Lamberville simply stated; "I send you a treasure, guard it well." If perplexed at first by the cryptic message, the priests soon found the meaning behind Father Lamberville's words; Kateri was indeed like no one that they had ever encountered before.

As with other members of her clan, Kateri continued the routines of her Mohawk people along with the liturgies and sacraments offered each day. Maintaining her hours of prayer and meditation, she also performed her daily tasks with care. She realized and honored what the Church teaches as the 'Little Way; the day to day chores are to be sanctified with love and dedication, nothing great or small was performed unless it was for Christ. Each task became altered by her intentions and her awareness that even such menial activities could bring her closer to God. By such, she knew her existence was not to be involved in grand deeds or adventures, but rather in those small duties with heroic virtue instead. When exhausted or ill, Kateri sought neither relief nor assistance, but took the road others before her had scorned, for she had glimpsed the welcoming embrace of Christ.

On a visit to Ville Marie (Montreal), she discovered nuns working in the hospitals, schools and living on for Christ. On her return to Sault, she requested to be able to enter such a convent, but at the time, the priest could not envision and Indian woman in the cloister. Undeterred, Kateri asked if she could take the vow of perpetual virginity, that was granted and on 25 March, 1679, kneeling motionless and oblivious to her surroundings, Kateri vowed to live as a Bride to Christ. Many suspected that solemn vow that day placed the seal on her life and she would not long be with them. Within the year, her health began to fail and she and confined to her bed, she waited with docile patience for the end. Administering the Eucharist and viaticum as her death approached, Kateri made a final request for to be clad in fine appeal than the well-worn and shabby garments she was usually clothed in, necessary she felt to meet her Bridegroom. Her last words; 'Iesos konoronkwa', 'Jesus, I love you.' Kateri Tekakwitha died in Wednesday of Holy Week, 17 April, 1680. As her eyes were closed, her body took on a lustrous radiance and the scars disappeared from her face, she was twenty-four years old. At that moment, two French trappers seeing the shining maiden, knelt and asked who she was, they were told Kateri Tekakwitha, they vowed to make a beautiful coffin for her. The message went out to all with no need to explain, 'The saint is dead.'

The principal relics of Kateri Tekakwitha are enshrined within a sealed marble tomb at Saint Francis Xavier Mission, now at Kahnawake, near Montreal, Canada. When the mission was moved, her remains were exhumed and moved as well. In the late 1800's, a monument was erected over her original burial site. The Native Americans began their devotions to Kateri Tekakwitha almost at once, and novenas were recited and Masses celebrated. She appeared to mission members soon after her death, and within months favors were reported as a result of her intercession.[11]

---

11 www,newadvent.org

In 1942, Pope Pius XII declared her Venerable, and Pope John Paul II declared her Blessed on June 22, 1980. She was also named as a patroness of World Youth Day 2002. On 21 October, 2012, Pope Benedict XVI canonized as Saint.

QUESTIONS

1. Though we have the example of Kateri, why do we tend to forget the value to honor and offer up the Little Way in our daily duties for Christ?
2. Why was Father Lamberville so troubled for Kateri?
3. Why did Father Lamberville find it odd to find a saint in the wilderness of Canada?
4. What causes the hatred for converts such as Kateri?
5. Why, when we are all called upon to be saints, we cannot hear as well as Kateri?

Chapter Five:
Faith from England: 1600-1634
The Conception of the Maryland Colony

The enormity of this expedition began with a sleight of hand by George Calvert, the first Lord of Baltimore and Sir Thomas Arundell. King James, though embracing the Church of England, did not entirely disregard his Catholic roots and granted Lord Baltimore a charter for territory north of Virginia, double of what is now the state of Maryland and encompassing all of Delaware and the southern boundary of Pennsylvania. (The whole grant extended the length of 15 miles wide by 138 miles long, and the fertile valley lying between the north and south branches of the Potomac River.)

He was descended from a noble Flemish family and born in Kipling, in Yorkshire in 1582. After receiving his Bachelor and Master of Arts from Oxford, he gained an appointment in Ireland and subsequently promoted to various other offices. It was said he kept a clear head, dispatched orders with prompt action and all his dealings were honest. Sir Robert Cecil, a minister under Elizabeth made him his chief clerk and when he became Lord High Treasurer, named Calvert clerk of the Privy Council. In 1617, at the age of twenty-five, George Calvert was knighted under James I, and amongst other favors befitting his new status, he was granted a large track of land in Ireland. Though what is also interesting to note, in 1609, being interested in colonizing America, Sir Calvert was one of the members of the Virginia Company of Planters, and fifteen years later; he was part of the council in England for the government of that province. In part with this, he purchased the southeastern peninsula of Newfoundland in 1620.

Four years after the self-proclaimed Puritans left on the Mayflower, Sir Calvert realized the inadequacies of the various religions proliferating outside of the proscribed for all England. To his mind, the dissenters were a confusion to the faith and Church of England, only a feeble attempt to retrieve a wrong course. All were found all wanting and with a decision which could have given him leave to join the ranks of those priests and laymen, who, as example for all those holding true to the One, Holy, Catholic and Apostolic Church, had been hanged, drawn and quartered for their faith, Sir Calvert with conviction, converted. Quite aware of the probable consequences of his actions and in full knowledge of the laws against Catholicism, he relinquished his seat in Parliament and announcing his commitment to King James I, he immediately resigned his post as Secretary of State. Contrary to the expected, King James, retained Sir Calvert as a member of the Privy Council and also regranted him his estates in Ireland, exempted him from the obligations, which as a Catholic he could not fulfill and as a reward for his long and faithful service, created him Baron of Baltimore in the kingdom of Ireland. In view of the possible and his return to the Church his forbearers brought to England, on 7 April, 1623, Sir Calvert obtained a charter for the province in Newfoundland, though only yet a landholder, the granting gave him sole proprietorship of the province.

Figure 1 (far right) Ferryland, New Foundland

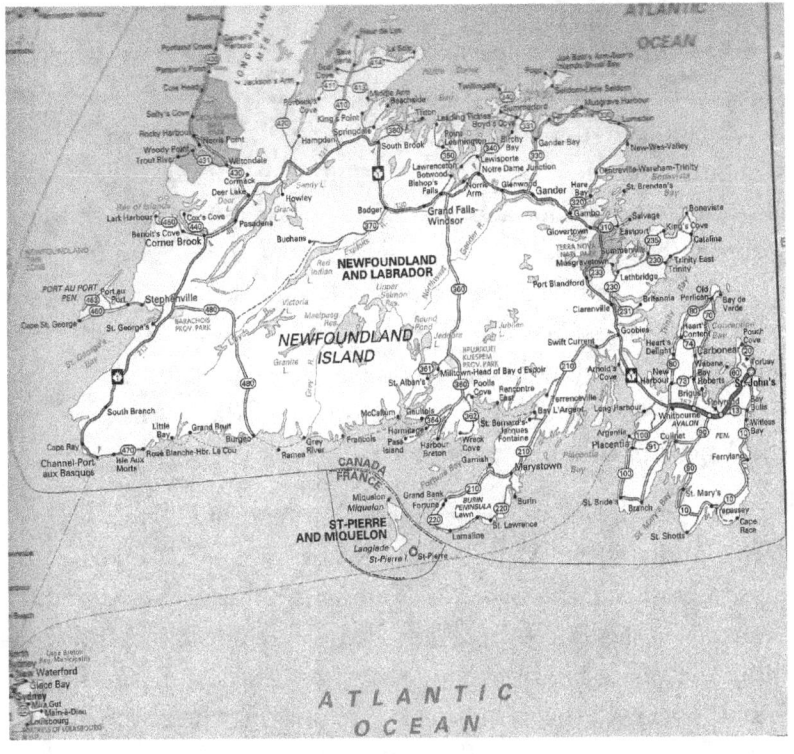

The envisioned plan was to create a haven for Catholics, as well as a place where all denominations could live without prosecution from any. 'The charter of Avalon made him true and absolute Lord and proprietary of the region, granted, which was erected into a province, with full power to make necessary laws, appoint officers, enjoy the patronage and advowson of all churches. Full authority was given to all the King's subjects to proceed to the province and settle there, notwithstanding any law to the contrary. The settlers were to be exempt from all taxation imposed by the king or his successors. It was provided that the laws should not be repugnant or contrary to those of England, and a special clause; 'Provided always that no interpretation bee admitted thereof (of the charter) whereby God's holy and true Christian religion or allegiance due to us, our heires and successors may in anything suffer any prejudice or diminution.'[12]

The remarkable aspects of the Avalon charter gave what the King James could not directly do or cede to to protect the Catholic religion, the underlying gave Catholics the ability to emigrate without hindrance, gave Lord Baltimore such laws as he pleased and with more importance, no power was required of him to enforce the penal codes against Catholics. But also, acting far ahead of his time, he gave equal liberty to all, regardless of their religious affiliations. Thus, for Catholics, the opportunity to hold lands, have their own churches and priests, gave and bequeathed to the persecuted, a foothold under the auspices of the English realm in the American colonies.

This first dream was short lived. On the eastern most point of Newfoundland, Ferryland's climate, was most inhospitable, most especially during the winter, a Protestant minister, Reverend, Mr. Stourton, returning to England, filed complaints that Lord Baltimore allowed Mass to be said, and with the acrimonious dealings with the French, the ideal proved discouraging and sending a ship south for supplies with Lady Baltimore, she came upon the Chesapeake Bay and anchored. In October of 1629, Lord Baltimore joined her at her urging and gave decision for the whole province to move hither.

The first difficulty encountered, centered on the acting governor, John Pott and one gentleman called Clayborne, both demanded for all to take the oath of supremacy, though they were assuming powers not given to the officials in Virginia, these only came through the treasurer and council in England. Interesting to realize, England was a least a three months sail back, baring storms, so powers wrongfully taken by those 'in charge' were unable to be

---

[12] John Gilmary. Shea. History of the Catholic Church in the United States, Colonial Days, New York, 1886 Pp. 30-31

refuted by any embarking on her shores for the length of time for an answer to return.

As of 1628, King James, no longer the King of England, Lord Baltimore wrote prior to leaving Newfoundland in August of 1629 to King Charles 1st, now King of England. (King James' brother) He was soliciting a grant for a precinet of land in Virginia and enjoy the same privileges he was granted in his first charter in the new world. Of which he was still much interested in. Trusting his family to God, he left them in Virginia and sailed for England, hoping his influence would obtain a new grant.

The viperous hatred arrived prior to Lord Baltimore and to the ears first of King Charles, the petitioned grant was rejected, the King realizing the value of political decorum in the realm. Though Lord Baltimore persisted and requested the lands north of Virginia so as to carry on his resolve and to be far enough away from Protestant England. This grant, a royal patent, was given, and the lands, now known as Maryland, were the first free Catholic colony under English rule in the America.

The succeeding plans go as God degrees, not to the want of man's strategy and devices. Before the charter had passed through the Great Seal of England, Lord Baltimore passed away. His son Cecil becomes the inheritor of his father's estates and titles and with that, of the greater importance, retained the charter, which was issued on 20 June, 1632 from King Charles I.

"The charter also contained the most comprehensive grant of civil and political authority and *jurisdiction* that ever emanated from the English Crown. It was a palatinate that was created with all the royal and viceregal *rights* pertaining to the unique and exceptional kind of government then existing in the Bishopric of *Durham*. The grantee appointed the governor and all the civil and military officers of the province. The writs ran in his name. He had power of life and death over the inhabitants as regards punishments for crime. He could erect manors, the grantees of which enjoyed all the *rights* and privileges belonging to that kind of estate in *England*. Many of them were created. He could confer titles of *honour* and thus establish a colonial aristocracy. Of all the territory embraced within the boundaries clearly set out in the charter, "the grantee, his heirs, successors and assigns, were made and constituted the *true* and absolute lords and proprietaries". [13]

Even when England was still Catholic, there was not a necessity for any such provisions to be mandated for the granting of such a charter. The extent under Charles I for this grant gave Maryland no royal charter beholden to the King for obedience to the laws of England; the enormity was freedom for Catholics since Henry the 8th chose to denounce the Pope.

To forbear from the vile tattling his father received from the Protestants who sailed with him to Newfoundland, Lord Cecil requested those of other denominations to choose and bring with them their own ministers. For their part they neither sought nor asked to have their own, even after several years in the colonies, they remained indifferent for their own religious ministrations. For the Catholic settlers, Lord Baltimore applied to Father Richard Blount, who at the time was the provincial for the Jesuits in England. He also wrote to the General of the Society in Rome, hoping to attract their zeal for an unknown land and willing to forgo the living support from their flock. (Though perhaps unbeknownst to Lord Baltimore, the Jesuits were quite familiar with the dangers of Catholic hostility in Virginia and the surrounding environs, coupled with the suspicions and violence of the Native Americans.) Two Fathers were assigned the title of gentlemen adventurers and taking with them artisans, acquired lands as did the others and from this they were to draw their personal sustenance.

---

13   www.newadvent.org

(There are however historical indications of financial wherewithal were furnished by Father Thomas Copley and their means to be maintained.)

Supplied and ready to sail, the Ark of 350 tons and the Dove of fifty tons, had received the warrants form the Lord Admiralty to embark with the provision; exempting the Catholics among his crew were not to be imprisoned for emigrating from the country. Further delays were created on false accusations to which the King's Bench issued the following.

'The charter to Cecilius was opposed by the agents of the Virginia colonists, on the ground that the grant was an encroachment on the territory of _Virginia_. This contention was untenable. For, by the judgment of the King's Bench in 1624, eight years before the issuing of the Baltimore Charter, in certain *quo warranto* proceedings instituted in the King's Bench, the Virginia colony was converted into a royal colony, and the king revested with the title to all the territory embraced in the charter of the _London_ or Virginia Company, with full power and authority to grant all or any part of it to whomsoever he pleased, which he subsequently freely exercised without question in the cases of the grants of _New Jersey_, _Pennsylvania_, the Carolinas and the northern neck of _Virginia_. The question was only raised as to the grant of Maryland, and that solely and avowedly because it was a grant to a _Catholic_ nobleman for the purpose of establishing a _Catholic_ colony. The committee of the Privy Council on American plantations, after a full hearing of both parties, unanimously decided, "to leave the Lord Baltimore to his charter, and the _Protestants_ to their remedy at law"[14].

Given free leave, the ships set sail on 22 November, 1633. The Jesuit Fathers were brought aboard from the Isle of Wright, as with several brothers and servants. All aboard both ships comprised of mainly Catholics, several Protestants who consisted of those neces-

---

14   www.newadvent.org.

sary to build a new colony in America. In all, 250 people joined Lord Baltimore on the voyage to share and carry on the vision of his father.

The Ark and the Dove entered through the Chesapeake and came to anchor at Point Comfort before sailing up the Potomac to Saint Clement. On 25 March, 1634 in the main bastion of the English colonies, catholicity was planted and consecrated by Christ's Cross.

"On the day of the Annunciation of the Blessed Virgin Mary in the year 1634", the *Jesuit Father Andrew White*, set down in his "Relatio Itineris in Marylandiam[15]", or "Narrative of the Voyage of The Ark and The Dove", "we celebrated the first Mass on that island (St. Clement's). This had never been done before in this part of the world." After the holy sacrifice, bearing on our shoulders a huge cross, which we had hewn from a tree, we moved in procession to a spot selected, the governor, commissioners and other Catholics, putting their hands first unto it and erected it as a trophy to Christ our Savior; then humbly kneeling, we recited with deep emotion, the Litany of the Holy Cross."

In advance of landing, while still sailing from England, Lord Baltimore set up instructions for their conduct while on the voyage and upon the settlement of their new province. Considering the journey, itself took four months and those aboard were of different creeds and rather cramped on two small vessels, Lord Calvert's missive stood up remarkably well.

"In this first article he enjoins, both on shipboard and on land, an abstinence from all religious controversies, "to preserve peace and unity amongst all the passengers and to suffer no *scandal* or offence, whereby just complaint may be made by them in Virginia or in *England* and to treat the *Protestants* with as much mildness and favor as *justice* will require[16]"

---

15   Relatio Itineris in Marylandiam

16   www.newadvent.org

To respect justice with the of the Piscataways, Lord Baltimore sailed up to the river of Saint Mary's to purchase the land he was given in the charter. The spot chosen lay a mile above the broad stream of Saint Mary's River, emptying into the Potomac twelve miles from its mouth. The village the Indians had erected, they were emigrating to the west, weary of the attacks by the Susquehanna tribe. The chief, Archihau, gave leave for the sale and the pilgrims of the Ark and the Dove took procession, renaming the town Saint Mary's.

Peace was engendered with the Native Americans with honor, Sir John Harvey, then Governor of Virginia was received as a welcome guest and the new settlement began with both Catholics and Protestants living together with the freedom of religion. There was none attempting to disparage, nor interfere with the others religious practices, the first conceived and practiced in the known world then.

QUESTIONS

1. In the face of the hostile and violent actions to Catholics in the early 1600's of England, how can we emulate George Calvert's bravery in his decision to convert to Catholicism?
2. By the same token, what reasons did the Protestants not endanger the voyage to the new colony, knowing it was to be Catholic?
3. Your father Lord Baltimore has just passed away and you are the inheritor of all his estates, most notably the charter. What would be your reactions and reasons to carry on the dream your father envisioned?
4. Why were such alleged difficulties created to bar the Ark and the Dove from leaving London?
5. Write a personal log of the voyage over, chose either ship.

Chapter Six:
The Life of the Maryland Colony 1634-1769

All boded well for the beginning, the Piscataways had left a few of their buildings behind, including an oblong oval barkhouse, which lodged the priests and served as the church. The sketch below is the one built after the first was burned down in 1644 by Claiborne and his force aided by Richard Ingle.

SITE OF THE CITY OF ST. MARY'S, MD., WHERE THE FIRST CATHOLIC CHAPEL WAS ERECTED. FROM A SKETCH BY GEORGE ALFRED TOWNSEND.

The climate far more congenial than Newfoundland and the soil fertile, coupled with the security, safety of the colonists, by the liberal conditions of Lord Baltimore, equality of religion and the freedom thereof, soon attracted numerous immigrants, and the colony grew, much to the anger of her Virginia neighbors. From the onset of their landing, Fathers White and Altham with the assistance of the lay brother Thomas Gervase, began their apostolic labors among their Protestant brethren first and the surrounding native tribes. The success came quicker with the Native Americans, than with the Protestant contingent. Tayac, chief of the Piscataways converted, as with his wife and many of their tribesmen. A princess from the Patuxents, along with several of her people and another neighboring tribe accepted the faith form the Fathers. For this, Father White wrote and prepared a grammar, dictionary and the catechism in the Piscataway language, which unfortunately was destroyed in the attack and capture of Saint Mary's by Richard Ingle in 1644.

Though the following was found in the law books from Massachusetts, she copied the text verbatim from Virginia. These laws were put in place soon after the arrival of the first colonists in Virginia.

"This Court taking into consideration the great wars and combustion which are this day in Europe, and that the same are observed to be chiefly raised and fomented by the secret practices of those of the Jesuitical order, for the prevention of like evils amongst ourselves, it is ordered by the authorities of this Court that no Jesuit or ecclesiastical person ordained by the authority of the pope shall henceforth come within our jurisdiction, and if any person shall give cause of suspicion that he is one of such society, he shall be brought before some of the magistrates, and if he cannot free himself of such suspicion, he shall be committed or bound on to the next Court of Assistants to be tried and proceeded with by banishment or otherwise, as the court shall see cause; and if any such person so banished shall be taken the second time within this jurisdiction, he shall upon lawful trial and conviction, be put to death.." ~during the French & Indian wars, Catholics were disarmed and heavily taxed and had to be registered so their movement could be tracked.

* Under Royal order in the Colonies, Catholics could not hold office.

* Irish immigrants were not admitted in the 18th Century to cut down on the number of Catholics in the colonies.
* In 1700 Catholic priests found in New York were subject to life imprisonment.
* In 1704, Maryland, which had the most Catholics, passed laws aimed at preventing the growth of Catholicism. Priests were prevented to make converts or baptize children of Protestant parents. Catholics were not allowed to teach in school. Irish servants were heavily taxed to stave off migration. They were not allowed to vote or hold office.
* 1755, also in Maryland, the property tax for Catholics was double what Protestants had to pay.
* In Virginia, Catholics could not vote or hold office and Catholic priests were not allowed in the colony. Nor could Catholics act as legal guardians or testify as witnesses.
* In 1756 when a war broke out between England & France, Virginia ruled that no Catholic could possess a gun or own a horse.
* A law on North Caroline books read: "full liberty of conscience to all, excluding Papists."[17]

The idyll before long was encroached by the unabated hostility of Maryland's, Virginia and the resentment and vengeance of William Claiborne. Being a member of the Government Council, Claiborne obtained a license from Governor Harvey to trade with the Dutch in Manhattan and those English in Newfoundland. To establish a trading post with convenience to himself and for an irritant to Lord Calvert, Claiborne chose Kent Island. He never acquired, nor requested leave to own any part of the land, he be-

---

17 In the Name of Heaven; 3000 Years of Religious Persecution, Engh, Mary Jane Prometheus Books, 2007

came a squatter on. The vantage point was excellent for trading vessels, refusing to acknowledge Lord Baltimore's charter and his authority and with a vigor, inciting local tribes against the Popish invasion; in all this, Claiborne had the backing of the Council of Virginia. The immediate response, Lord Baltimore took possession of Kent Island. This time without sanction, Claiborne organized a force to retake the island, but was met by the force from Maryland under the command of Captain Cornwaleys. Claiborne's Virginians were defeated, but he escaped and from then on stayed the unrelenting enemy of the Catholic colonists. His threats, never idle, he once again in 1644, descended upon Saint Mary's having instigated Richard Ingle bore down on the province in the vessel Reformation, ousting Lord Baltimore, several principal families and two Jesuit Fathers to flee to Virginia. With the capture of the town complete, they burned Saint Mary's, destroyed all the valuable records, pillages the houses and as a final act, desecrated and destroyed the chapels of the missionaries. Father White remaining behind was captured and sent back to England in chains to stand trial, for the indictment for any Catholic priest, returning was an offense for which death is the sentence. Father White however pleaded that his arrival was not voluntary and was able to escape the dictates of the law.

The specific aim of course was the destruction and elimination of the Catholic colony. Once again, Claiborne and his Virginian brethren failed in their object, Lord Baltimore's brother, Leonard Calvert as Governor, had proceeded to reclaim by bringing a small force and drove out the marauders from Saint Mary's City and thus re-establishing his authority. Even with this, Cecilius Calvert was having a time in constant confrontations with his enemies who notwithstanding their recent loses, was seeking to abolish and annihilate any semblance of papacy in the English New World; another controversy caused him to assert his Proprietary over his own Jesuits.

The dispute centered on the gift of a track of land given to the priests by their Indian converts. Lord Baltimore took umbrage since the acceptance came without his knowledge or consent and which he felt violated his rights under the express provisions of the charter. He consequently demanded the surrounding of the land, which the Jesuits refused to comply with his orders. For several years it was an acrimonious wrangle until the Father General of the order sided with Lord Baltimore. It was not so much the acquisition by the good fathers, but rather the manner and method by which the land was acquired. But to augment the objections, Lord Baltimore, in 1651 set aside 10,000 acres of land near Calverton Manor for the benefit of the Native converts which he put under the care and the direction of the Fathers. It became the first fund established within the English possessions in America for the support of Indian missions. Outside of the land squabble, peace and prosperity came to the colony and Maryland began to grow in population and in wealth. Though no specific statistics are available of the number of inhabitants during this period, (1645), the estimate is between four and five thousand individuals, of which three-fourths were Catholic. These individuals held the majority of governing offices and the bulk of the legislative body, until the Puritan Rebellion in 1650. The original Jesuit Fathers, Andrew White, Thomas Copley (alias Philip Fisher), Ferdinand Poulton, (alias John Brock and Morgan) attended to all the Maryland colony and converted almost all of the Protestant colonists who journey with them on the Ark and the Dove. Also the many new arrivals from England and Virginia. In regards to the pending resolution on the difficulty between Lord Baltimore and the Fathers, four Franciscans arrived, but peace restored, they retired leaving the field to the Jesuits.

In a remarkable piece of legislation, in 1649 the General Assembly passed the celebrated Toleration Act. "Under a provision in the charter giving to the Lords Baltimore the initiation of legislation in the province, *Cecilius Calvert* had drawn up a body of *laws* sixteen in number, to be adopted by the Assembly, and among them was this famous Act. It was passed by that body, the majority of whom mere *Catholics*, without a dissenting voice. "And whereas", it reads, "the enforcing of the *conscience* in matters of religion hath frequently fallen out to be of dangerous consequence in those commonwealths where it hath been practiced, and for the more quiet and peaceable government of the province and the better to preserve mutual *love* and amity amongst the inhabitants thereof: Be it therefore enacted that noe *person* or *persons* whatsoever within this province. . .professing to *believe* in *Jesus Christ*, shall henceforth be in any waies troubled, molested or discountenanced for or in respect of his or her religion or in the free exercise thereof within this province nor in anything compelled to the *belief* or exercise of any other religion against his or her consent." The act then provides penalties for violation of its provisions. In the controversies about this celebrated Act of Toleration, efforts have been made by many *Protestant* writers to deprive *Cecilius Calvert* of the merit of its authorship, but the judgment of all fair historians gives to *Cecilius Calvert*, and to him alone, following the example of his *father*, the *honour* of "being the first in the annals of mankind", as Bancroft says in his "History of the United States", "to make religious freedom the basis of the State".[18]

From the English point of view, the solution was simple, *Cecilius Calvert* needed only to renounce his faith and swear allegiance to the Crown and the Church of England. Then and only then would all persecution cease, but he was a conscientious *Catholic* and the requirements demanded, he refused. Therefore, in 1643, the House of Burgesses of Virginia passed a stringent law requiring of all *persons* a strict conformity with the worship and discipline of the *Church of England*, the established Church of that colony. The governor in particular put this act into vigorous execution, and a

---

18   *www.newadvent.org* and Cecilius Calvert

considerable number of _Puritans_ were driven out of _Virginia_ into Maryland. At their pleading, the Governor set aside a large tract of land on the Severn, where they made a settlement, calling it Providence (now Annapolis). Not long after, ungracious of the gift, they began to complain that their consciences would not allow them to acknowledge the authority of a _Catholic_ proprietary. Their return for asylum: started a rebellion in 1650 and seized the government of the colony. They immediately convened their own a General Assembly in which _Catholics_ were declared ineligible as either members or electors. Of paramount importance, though without any legal standing, this illegal and revolutionary body repealed the Act of Toleration of 1649, and to 'enact' another "Concerning Religion" which specifically contained this provision: "That none who profess and exercise the Papistic, commonly known as the _Roman Catholic_ religion, can be protected in this province." By this act, _Catholics_ and those who professed the _Church of England_ were in equal standing of being against the Puritan laws of the colony they without right overthrew

For the next eight years, the _Catholic Church_ suffered much under the Puritan usurpation. Under this lawless governing body, self-ruled gangs flaunted the province and desecrated _chapels_ mission houses and destroying the _property_ of Catholics. By their acts, three of the _Jesuit priests_ fled to _Virginia_, where they kept themselves in hiding for two or three years, enduring great privations. One only remained in Maryland enduring the ridicule of those in power. At last in 1658 the government of the province was restored to Lord Baltimore and the General Assembly was reconvened and re-enacted the Toleration Act of 1649. This Act remained on the statute book under the _Catholic_ proprietaries until the _Protestant Revolution of 1689_. Maryland enjoyed again another era of quiet and prosperity, and the _Jesuits_ returning to the province resumed their missionary labors. In 1660 the population of the province numbered 12,000; in 1665, 16,000; and in 1671, 20,000. This rapid increase is a _proof_ of the wisdom and liberality of the proprietary's rule. The _Catholic_ inhabitants during this period, the majority of whom were in St. Mary's and Charles Counties, were estimated to be between 4000 and 5000, served by two, sometimes three, _Jesuits_ and two _Franciscans_ who arrived in 1673.

Philip Calvert, brother of Cecilius, was governor from 1660 to 1662, when he was succeeded by _Charles Calvert_, the son and heir of Cecilius, who, on the death of his _father_ in 1675, became the third Lord Baltimore and second proprietary of the province. Charles married and settled in the province, and lived there several years, discharging the _duties_ of governor as well as of proprietary according to liberal and enlightened principles and with consideration for the welfare of the inhabitants. In 1683 the General Assembly voted him 100,000 lbs. of tobacco as an expression of "the _duty_ gratitude and affection" of the people of the province. This he declined on the ground that it would impose too great a tax burden on the people.

Even within this peace, the troubles continued. Constant attempts were made in 1676 to force him into making public provisions for the _clergymen_ of the _Church of England_. Following his _father's_ example, he refused such orders, and with the approval of the inhabitants, who all knew of the worthless character and _scandalous_ conduct of most of the _ministers_ of that denomination sent over from _England_. Therefore without authority, in 1676, the _Protestant_ malcontents issued a proclamation, denouncing the government of the _Catholic_ Proprietary, demanding its extinction, and for the appointment of a royal governor. They assembled in arms in Calvert County to carry out their program, but Governor Notley, in the absence of _Sir Charles Calvert_ in _England_, quickly suppressed the movement and hanged two of the ringleaders. Later on the malcontents availed themselves of the opportunity created by the _Revolution in England_ to raise the standard of revolt against the government of Lord Baltimore, and to call upon all good _Protestants_ to aid in its overthrow. Under the leadership of one John Coode, an _apostate Catholic_, a Colonel Jowles and others formed "The Protestant Association in arms to defend the Protestant religion". All sorts of lying charges against the _Catholics_ were scattered throughout the community, among the accusations, they were accused of forming an alliance with the Indians for the massacre of the _Protestants_. The Government of the proprietary again overthrown, and a Committee of Public Safety was installed in its place. This Committee appealed to William and Mary for recognition, and to their discredit, these monarchs acquiesced.

No single sustaining charge of offense was ever brought against Lord Baltimore (Charles, son of Cecilius) in the legal sense, except the most damning one, he was a _Catholic_. Without a trial by a jury of his peers, and notwithstanding the commendations of several high-ranking _Protestants_ in several counties, Lord Baltimore was deprived of all the civil and political authority that had been in direct violation of the standing conferred upon him in the charter. And by royal degree, it remained so until his death in 1715. Yet, although stripped of his proprietary rank, William and Mary refused to sanction the repeated attempts made by the Maryland usurpers to rob him of his _property rights_. These _rights_ he retained able to administer his land office, appointing his surveyors, collecting his rents and issuing, as the only recognized source of title, grants and patents for lands to claimants under the conditions of plantation _promulgated_ by his _father_ Cecilius. It was this retention of his territory, which enabled Lord Baltimore to prevent the future State of Maryland from absorption to either the colonies of Virginia or _Pennsylvania_.

Disregarding the original provisions of the charter, of which the proprietary was no bound to England, William and Mary and reestablishing it as a royal colony, appointed Lionel Copley governor. Thus began with renewed vigor the reign of religious intolerance and bigotry. The 'cause', encouraged by the Government of _En-_

gland and the colony, gained fervor with the sympathy and support of the *Protestant* inhabitants of Maryland.

Since the illegal revoking of the Maryland Charter, the "Act of Religion" in 1692 was only redundant since the penal laws against Catholics, was still in force in England and all English colonies. This Act reiterated that the *Church of England* as the *Church* of the province, demanded conformity with its worship and discipline. The Episcopal *clergymen* were given the *jurisdiction* in the testamentary causes, though the members of the *Church of England* in Maryland at that time constituted but a small minority of the people. For the Dissenters and the *Quakers*, who with the *Catholics*, formed the majority of the people, the act caused great concern and distress.

The differences are quite between the governances of the English and the Catholic proprietaries. First, there was no Establish Church, no tax imposed for its support, no conformity with its worship and discipline required under penalties for non-compliance. Yet the Act of 1692 and the other passed in 1702 re-enforced the demarcation lines, though the second Act exempted *Puritans* and *Quakers* and all other Dissenters from the provisions of this *law*, except the annual tax of 40 pounds of tobacco per poll on all the inhabitants for the support of the Establishment. For the *Catholics*, they and they alone remained subject to the pains, penalties, disabilities, and taxes provided in this Act. The most onerous was the Test Oath of 1692 for which *Catholic* attorneys were debarred from practicing in the provincial courts. By the Act of 1704 *Catholics* were prohibited from practicing their religion; *priests* were debarred from the exercise of their functions; *priests* and *parents* forbidden to teach *Catholic* children their religion, and the children encouraged to refuse obedience to the rule and authority of their *parents*. Also in 1715 a law was adopted providing that if a *Protestant* should die leaving a *widow* and children, and such *widow* should marry a *Catholic*, or be herself of that opinion, it should be the _duty_ of the governor and council to remove such child or children out of the custody of such _parents_ and place them where they might be securely _educated_ in the _Protestant religion_.

To add more injury on the death of Charles, Lord Baltimore, in February, 1715, His son Benedict Leonard now succeeded to the title and estates. This son, years prior to his father's death, had renounced the _Catholic Faith_, and with his _family_ conformed to the _Church of England_. His father, incensed by his son's dishonoring the work of three generations, cut off his allowance and perhaps disowned Benedict and his family. Now in need for a replacement of funds, he appealed to Queen Anne who directed Governor Hart to provide for him an annuity of £500 out of the revenue of the province. This precedent proved further injurious to Catholics, for Benedict died 5 April, 1715. His son Charles II, who had conformed with his _father_, became the fifth Lord Baltimore and the fourth proprietary, and received from Queen Anne the government of the province. In consequence of relinquishing the Catholic faith, Charles II added in 1718 a more stringent law to pass. It barred _Catholics_ from the exercise of the franchise and the holding of any office in the province. This Act was amended and re-enacted again 1729 which in the cases of widows with children professing the faith, gave power to take any child or children to any _justice_ of the county court. This was done regardless to the sex or age of the child or children; they were placed wherever the _justice_ pleased. There was no appeal for Catholics.

Even to the eve of the American Revolution, none of these 'laws' were ever rescinded and as with Henry the 8th, any lands owned by any Catholic religious, became the property of the Crown. Since Cecilius, the _Jesuits_ owned and cultivated several large manors and other tracts of fertile lands, the revenues of which were devoted to religion, charity, _education_, and their missionary work. For this the Assembly was petitioned to enact that all manors, tenements, etc., possessed by the _priests_ should on 1 October, 1756, be taken from them, and vested in a commission appointed for that purpose and sold. The proceeds of the sale were to be devoted to the protection of the Protestants from the French and Indians. Priests were now as ever required to take all the test _oaths_ and if they refused, banishment, and, as considered "Romish recusants", their lands were to be forfeited.

As with England, two houses comprised the governing aspects of the colony. The Upper House was the Governor's Council which framed a bill, titling it "To prevent the growth of Popery within this province", explicitly stating; _priests_ were to be made incapable of holding any lands, to be _obliged_ to register their names, and give bond for their good conduct, were prohibited from converting any _Protestants_ under the penalty of high treason, and further that any _person educated_ at a foreign _Catholic seminary_ could not inherit or hold lands in the province. . But a controversy arose over agreement between the two Houses and the bill during was dropped, yet to render the province a place no longer a desirable for residence to loyal _Catholic_ gentleman and their _families_ was the only object of these propositions and _laws_. At this point Charles Carroll, who later was a key signer for the Declaration of Independence, wrote to his son that Maryland was no longer a fit place for a _Catholic_ to reside, and he felt the necessity to dispose of his great landed estate and leave the province. His son in response persuaded him not to do so. There were some _families_ who sought the refuge of _Pennsylvania_ from these intolerant _laws_ and the more intolerant sentiments of the people. In 1752 the same Charles Carroll, after consultation with some of the principal _Catholic families_ of Maryland, went to _France_ to obtain from Louis XV a tract of land in the Louisiana territory for the purpose of transporting the _Catholics_ of the province in a body to that country. His mission failed and the Maryland _Catholics_ began to _emigrate_ to Kentucky in 1774, and in 1785 twenty-five _Catholic families_ set out from St. Mary's County for Pottinger's Creek. It appeared for the time George Calvert's dream was to be extinguished for good.

To understand the effects the laws against Catholics, equate the results in the population of the colony. For an equivalent, consider the number of parishes in a large city of today. By 1754 the population stood at 153,000, of Catholics numbered about 8000. The priest, usually exclusively Jesuits numbered four to five. They rose to ten to twelve by the end of the decade. According to Bishop Challoner, _vicar apostolic_ in _England_, in 1756, places the number of _priests_ at twelve. In 1763 the _Catholic_ population was estimated to be between 8000 and 10,000, whose spiritual needs were supplied by fourteen _Jesuits_. By 1769 this population had increased to 12,000. The number of conversions had increased.

By the time the Continental Congress voted for the Declaration of Independence and the subsequent following of the Revolution, put an end to the royal authority over the American colonies, and to the proprietary rule in Maryland. The result the English penal laws were stuck against Catholics and a new order of government was to prevail. Yet, there was Daniel Dulany, being an eminent lawyer and the attorney general of the province under the last proprietary governor, addressed a letter to the people of Maryland urging them to remain steadfast in their loyalty to the King of _England_ and to the provincial authority. He used the one aspect of the original charter to persuade his point to the colonists of Maryland from joining her sister colonies in the revolt. Under Section XX of the Maryland Charter the province enjoyed the right of absolute exemption from all taxation by king or Parliament. The authority of Mr. Dulany carried great weigh and his argument, well placed and strong. Another letter, calculated to exert added influence against to the patriot cause, was that the royal authority in Maryland only to a limited extent. Mr. Dulany went on to state that no royal governors had been appointed except during the usurpation of the _Protestant_ ascendency, and only when the government of the province, and the appointment of governors, was taken temporarily out of the hands of Charles, Lord Baltimore, because he was a *Catholic*. What he did not understand was that the proprietary rule, notwithstanding the anger of the malcontents and *revolutionists of 1689*, was acceptable to the people. The only ground of objection, indeed, ever urged against the government of either *Cecilius* or *Charles Calvert* was that they were *Catholics*.

QUESTIONS

1. Then as now, oaths are required to follow the dictates of a government, how can we stay so embolden to refuse the secular and maintain our faith?
2. Why is our allegiance to the Pope condemned as evil?
3. In the face of constant persecution, why did Lord Baltimore adhere to the faith and refuse to become a Protestant?
4. Explain the reasons for the Protestant Revolution of 1689.
5. Did the years prior to the Revolution change the attitude of persecution towards the Catholics?

Chronological History of Religious Influence in the New World and Europe (1600-1700)

* 1600: Pope *Clement VIII* sanctions use of coffee despite petition by priests to ban the Muslim drink as "the devil's drink". The Pope tried a cup and declared it "so delicious that it would be a pity to let the infidels have exclusive use of it. We shall cheat Satan by baptizing it."[10]
* 1614: *Tokugawa Ieyasu* bans Christianity from Japan.

* April 19, 1622: _Pope Gregory XV_ makes Armand Jean du Plessis de Richelieu a cardinal upon the nomination of _King Louis XIII_ – becoming _Cardinal Richelieu_. His influence and policies greatly impact the course of European politics.
* November 18, 1626: _Pope Urban VIII_ solemnly dedicates the New Basilica of St. Peter 1,300 years after the first Constantinian basilica was consecrated by _Pope Sylvester I_.
* 1633: Trial of _Galileo_, after which he is sentenced to _house arrest_.
* 1638: _Shimabara Rebellion_ leads to a further repression of Catholics, and all Christians, in Japan.
* 1653: The _Coonan Cross Oath_ was taken by a group of _Saint Thomas Christians_ against the Portuguese.
* September 12, 1683: _Battle of Vienna_. Decisive victory of the army of the _Holy League_, under King _John III Sobieski_ of Poland, over the Ottoman Turks, under Grand Vizier Merzifonlu _Kara Mustafa_ Pasha. The Turks do not threaten Western Europe militarily again.
* 1685: _Louis XIV_ revokes the _Edict of Nantes_, and large numbers of _Huguenot_ refugees leave France.
* 1691: _Pope Innocent XII_ declares against _nepotism_ and _simony_.

Chapter Seven:
The Revolutionary War Catholics

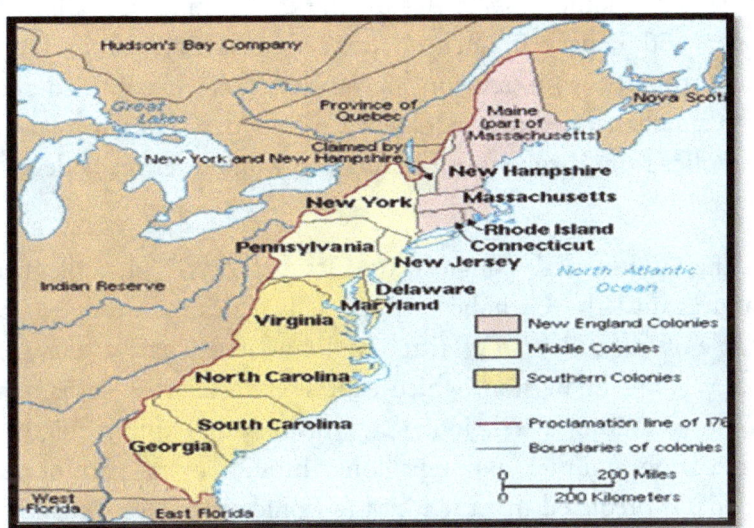

The Original Thirteen Colonies

The prelude of coalescing only some thirty percent of the colonists was and is most certainly the Declaration of Independence, yet there was vital factor little spoken of in the annuals stating the historical causes for the American Revolution, Britain's passing of the Quebec Act in1774. The effects of the 'Intolerable Acts', as they came to be called, onerous in their own right, yet none

---

19   Abitadeacon: The Catholic reality in Colonial America abitadeacon.blogspot.com/2012/07/catholic-reality-in-colonial

than the passage of this Act bound the colonies in such a vitriolic and united front against England. From the perceived absolute betrayal by Great Britain in granting religious freedom to Canada's Catholics, the founding fathers response came with swift and immediate ferocity; the quotes are as follows verbatim.

The evidence is made quite clear in the words of Alexander Hamilton and John Jay as seeing the Quebec Act as a diabolical threat. "Does not your blood run cold to think that an English Parliament should pass an Act for the establishment of arbitrary power and Popery in such an extensive country?...Your loves, your property, your religion are all at stake." He warned that the Canadian tolerance in Quebec would draw, like a magnet, Catholics from throughout Europe who would eventually destroy America.

The Continental Congress, on October 21, 1774, took their stand against the Catholic menace. It issued an address "to the People of Great Britain", written by John Jay, Richard Henry Lee and William Livingston, which expressed shock that Parliament would promote a religion that "disbursed impiety, bigotry, persecution, murder and rebellions through every part of the world." It predicted that the measure would encourage Canadians to "act with hostility against the free Protestant colonies, whenever a wicked Ministry shall choose to direct them." Once Americans were converted to Catholicism, they would be enlisted in a vast Popish army to enslave English Protestants.

In the late 1760s and early 1770s, colonists celebrated Anti-Pope Days, an anti-Catholic festival derived from the English Guy Fawkes day (named for a Catholic who attempted to assassinate King James I). "Orations, cartoons, and public hangings of effigies depicted royal ministers as in league alternately with the pope and the devil," writes historian Ruth Bloch.

Roger Sherman and other members of Continental Congress wanted to prohibit Catholics from serving in the Continental Army. Samuel Adams echoed the sentiment of the time by declaring in 1768: "I did verily believe, as I do still, that much more is to be dreaded from the growth of popery in America, than from the Stamp Act, or any other acts destructive of civil rights." [20]

This appalled and terrified many, if not all the colonists, into declaring this to be a British attempt to subjugate them religiously by allowing the detestable Catholics to expand into the colonies. Colonial newspapers railed against the Popish threat. The Pennsylvania Gazette said the legislation would now allow "these dogs of Hell" to "erect their Heads and triumph within our Borders." The Boston Evening Post reported that the step was "for the execution of this hellish plan" to organize 4,000 Canadian Catholics for an attack on America. In Rhode Island, every single issue of the Newport Mercury from October 2, 1774 to March 20, 1775 contained "at least one invidious reference to the Catholic religion of the Canadians," according to historian Charles Metzger. Protestant clergy fanned the flames. Rev. John Lathrop of the Second Church in Boston said Catholics "had disgraced humanity" and "crimsoned a great part of the world with innocent blood." Rev. Samuel West of Dartmouth declared the pope to be "the second beast" of Revelation while Joseph Perry warned his Connecticut neighbors that they would soon need to swap "the best religion in the world" for "all the barbarity, trumpery and superstition of popery; or burn at the stake, or submit to the tortures of the inquisition." And, he reasoned, English lawmakers were being controlled by the devil; the Quebec Act "first sprang from that original wicked politician." Commenting on anti-Catholic fervor, historian Alan Heimert wrote that there was "a special and even frenetic urgency to their efforts to revive ancient prejudices by announcing that the Quebec Act—

---

20 Speech to Congress; Samuel Adams 1768 The Catholic Church in Colonial America by Dr. Marian T. Horvat, Ph.D., 'Let None Dare Call it Liberty'

and it alone—confronted America with the possibility of the 'scarlet whore' soon riding 'triumphant over the heads of true Protestants, making multitudes drunk with the wine of her fornications.' The 1774 Pope Day was one of the grandest in years; in Newport, two large effigies of the pope were paraded. In New York, a group marched to the financial Exchange carrying a huge flag inscribed, "George III Rex, and the Liberties of America. No Popery." Later that day, a pamphlet that had been distributed urging tolerance toward the Catholics of Canada was smeared with tar and feathers and nailed to the pillory.

The silversmith and engraver Paul Revere created a cartoon for the Royal American Magazine called "The Mitred Minuet." It depicted four contented-looking mitred Anglican Bishops, dancing a minuet around a copy of the Quebec Act to show their "approbation and countenance of the Roman religion." Standing nearby are the authors of the Quebec Act, while a Devil with bat ears and spiky wings hovers behind them, whispering instructions. Within this atmosphere of emotional superstition, General Washington called out the Continental Congress on their foolish condemnation without first realizing the necessity of requesting support from France, a predominately-Catholic country. While Boston was glorifying in their 'Pope Day' in excess, Canada was receiving a delegation from the fledgling colonies for an appeal for neutrality. Among the representatives joining Benjamin Franklin and Samuel Chase on their unsuccessful attempt, were Charles Carroll, the only Catholic signer of the Declaration of Independence and his cousin John Carroll, a Jesuit prior to the suppression of the order, continued to be one of the colonies few priests, (In 1789, became the first American Bishop.) [21] Canada was not thrilled of the written protestations to England.

From this vitriolic hatred, the colonies' Catholics remained caught in the quandary, not of loyalties, as all are Catholic first be-

---

21 *www.catholichistory.net/Spotlights/SpotlightFounding.htm*

fore country, but the very real choice of conviction in the face of what John Highham described as "the most luxuriant, tenacious tradition of paranoiac agitation in American history". and Historian *Arthur Schlesinger Sr.* has called "the deepest-held bias in the history of the American people[22]." for a country and government quite willing to eradicate their religion and themselves. The decision remained, stay loyal to England, which was a short thirteen years away from passing the Catholic Relief Act or bear the worst of prejudicial brunt and fight with the colonists for independence. For by 1776, Catholics formed approximately 1.6% of the 2.5 million population of the thirteen colonies. The reasoning in hindsight is to conclude no viable purpose for Catholics to support the revolution, yet perhaps the persuasive power of Washington over the objections of the Continental Congress and the populace was such that the principles were worthy to defend. And also the realization without the support of France and Spain, both Catholic countries, the fight would come to a very ignoble end. (As an example, Massachusetts sent a chaplain to the French fleet when they arrived in Boston Harbor and the first Mass held in Boston was for a French soldier with members of the Continental Congress in attendance. Washington was also know to attend Mass. When another docked in Newport, Rhode Island, that colony repealed its act of 1664 that refused citizenship to Catholics.) But for France especially, there were other components and considerations involved, the recent loss to England in the French and Indian War and whether the colonies could prove themselves as an effective fighting force to defeat the British. The Battle of Saratoga in 1778 became the deciding factor and the first officer to join was the Count Marquis de Lafayette, (a Catholic). From the other foreign officers who served, either as soldiers of fortune in the American army or with the French allies, put the Revolution in debt to Catholics, including Polish captain *Tadeusz Kosciuszko* who as a colonel in Washington's army, fought in and made

---

22   *en.wikipedia.org/wiki/Anti-Catholicism*

important contributions at Ticonderoga and Saratoga. Another Pole, _Casismir Pulaski_, led Washington's cavalry, and died in the battle for Savannah. Also _Casimir Pulaski from Poland_, _De Grasse_, _Jean-Baptiste Donatien de Vimeur, Comte de Rochambeau_, and _Charles Hector, Comte d'Estaing_.[48]

Though often not recognized for their vital contributions, Spain also sent her part of own fleet, enlisting in the American Cause as well as supplies and money sent from Havana. Jordi Farragut Mesquida, the father of Admiral Farragut of Civil War fame, an immigrant from Spain, he served in the Revolution as both a naval officer and as a volunteer at the Battle of Cowpens. The value of Spain's formable Navy blocked England from the Mississippi Valley and harassed the British Navy throughout the Gulf of Mexico and the Caribbean Sea. On the Atlantic side was the Irish native John Barry. Enlisting American merchantmen, Barry who captained a number of vessels during the war was able to pester and run the English blockades. Another Catholic, John Barry Kelly wrote; 'Barry's war contributions are unparalleled: he was the first to capture a British war vessel on the high seas; he captured two British ships after being severely wounded in a ferocious sea battle; he quelled three mutinies; he fought on land at the Battles of Trenton and Princeton; he captured over 20 ships including an armed British schooner in the lower Delaware; he authored a Signal Book which established a set of signals used for effective communication between ships; and he fought the last naval battle of the American Revolution aboard the frigate Alliance in 1783. Barry was George Washington's choice to head the United States Navy when the president created it in 1794.'

23

In what is now southwestern Indiana, _Father Pierre Gibault,_ a missionary of French descent met with the Virginia militia under Colonel George Rogers Clark when they entered the area. It was Gibault and others meeting with the American commander and pledged their support of the region to the forces of independence in return for assurances of religious freedom. Even though this action was against the wishes of the bishop of Quebec, Gibault led the French residents of the Vincennes region in cooperating with the Americans regardless.

Another notable Catholic was nurse _Mary Waters,_ whose work in the patriot hospitals drew the praise of Founding Father (and physician) Benjamin Rush. The Philadelphia merchant _Stephen Moylan_ became Quartermaster General of the Continental Army and later raised a regiment of Pennsylvanians.

Though not all Catholics were revolutionaries, there was the Roman Catholic Volunteers who formed a military unit. Also the

---

23   Photos, from top: Independence Hall; Boston Massacre; George Rogers Clark's March on Vincennes; John Barry; Flag Raised at Independence Hall. All courtesy of National Archives and Records Administration (unrestricted)

New York-based Volunteers of Ireland was another regiment made up of Catholics fighting for King George. Alsace-born Joseph Cauffman, a prominent citizen of Philadelphia, remained loyal to England—though his son, Joseph, Jr., served the forces of independence as a medical doctor.

Throughout the war, the Vatican remained neutral and Catholics were free to choose sides. The conservative and anti-revolutionary, believed that their loyalty lay with Great Britain, while many other Catholics felt that the Crown had forfeited Americans' allegiance through tyranny.

Though Catholics could be found on both sides of the conflict, the experience of fighting side-by-side with Romanists, the witness of important patriots such as the Carrolls, and the valuable support of France and Spain, convinced many of the Revolutionaries that Catholics were not the horrors they were perceived to be.

There was Thomas Fitzsimons, who already distinguished himself as a soldier and leader during the Revolution. A native Irishmen, he became an important Philadelphia merchant who won election to an early Revolutionary government post in the face of laws barring Catholics from holding office.

Daniel Carroll had served in the Continental Congress and had signed the Articles of Confederation as well. At the constitutional convention, he championed ideas such as popular election of senators and reserving to the states all powers not explicitly delegated to the federal government.[24]

Even though the anti-Catholic feeling was beginning to ebb, it

---

24   www.catholichistory.net/people/events

was hardly eradicated, for after Arnold's treason, Arnold himself issued this proclamation, "Address to officers and soldiers of Continental army. *'What is America now but a land of widows, orphans, and beggars?–and should the parent nation cease her exertions to deliver you, what security remains to you even for the enjoyment of the consolations of that religion for which your fathers braved the ocean, the heathen, and the wilderness? Do you know that the eye which guides this pen lately saw your mean and profligate Congress at mass for the soul of a Roman Catholic in Purgatory, and participating in the rites of a Church, against whose antichristian corruptions your pious ancestors would have witnessed with their blood.*"[25]

The thought, was that England was behind this speech in an attempt to revive again revile for Popery. Little came from it as is evidenced on 4 July, 1779 when the French Minister Gerard extended an invitation to the Congress for a Te Deum Mass at Saint Mary's in Philadelphia for American Independence. (Interesting to note is that throughout the revolution, priests remained under the jurisdiction of the Bishop of the London District. After the war, Rome made entirely new arrangements for the creation of an American diocese under American bishops.)[26]

After the War, Washington paid tribute to the role Catholics played in the American Revolution: '*As mankind become more liberal they will be more apt to allow that all those who conduct themselves as worthy members of the community are equally entitled to the protection of civil government. I hope ever to see America among the foremost nations in examples of justice and liberality. And I presume that your fellow-citizens will not forget the patriotic part which you took in the accomplishment of their Revolution, and the establishment of their government; or the important assistance which they received from a nation in which the Roman Catholic faith is professed.*'

---

25   CATHOLICS AND THE American Revolution BY MARTIN I. J. GRIFFIN

26   *American Revolution and aftermath (1776–1800)*

John Carroll, first American bishop and a cousin of the Catholic signer of the Declaration of Independence, summed up Catholic participation in the Revolution: '*Their blood flowed as freely (in proportion to their numbers) to cement the fabric of independence as that of any of their fellow-citizens: They concurred with perhaps greater unanimity than any other body of men, in recommending and promoting that government, from whose influence America anticipates all the blessings of justice, peace, plenty, good order and civil and religious liberty.*'[27]

Catholic participation in the founding did not end with the cessation of hostilities with Britain. *Thomas Fitzsimons* and *Daniel Carroll* (John's brother) were Constitutional Convention delegates from Pennsylvania and Maryland, respectively. They are the two Catholics whose names are affixed to the United States Constitution.

Four years after the United States Constitution, the First Amendment was ratified in 1791; including the wording specifically, "Congress shall make no law respecting an establishment of religion, or prohibiting the free exercise thereof..." This amendment officially granted freedom of religion to all American citizens, and began the eventual repeal of all anti-Catholic laws from the statute books of all of the new American states. Regardless, some of America's *Founding Fathers* maintained their anti-clerical beliefs and stance. In 1788, *John Jay* urged the *New York Legislature* to require office-holders to renounce foreign authorities "*in all matters ecclesiastical as well as civil.*" *Thomas Jefferson* wrote, "*History, I believe, furnishes no example of a priest-ridden people maintaining a free civil government,*" and that "*In every country and in every age, the priest has been hostile to liberty. He is always in alliance with the despot, abetting his abuses in return for protection to his own.*"[28]

Though prejudice was contained, the Jesuit Fathers under the leadership of John Carroll, S.J. called several meetings of the cler-

---

27   11the-american-catholic.com/.../fortnight-for-freedom-day-eleven-cath...

28   en.wikipedia.org/wiki/Anti-Catholicism

gy for the purpose of organizing the Catholic Church in America being their first priority immediately following the treaty with England. These meetings, called the General Chapters, were held at White Marsh Plantation in 1783 which is now Sacred Heart Church in Bowie, MD. Deliberations led to the appointment of John Carroll by the Vatican as Prefect Apostolic, and making him superior of the missionary church in the thirteen states, the first plans for Georgetown University were also set up at this time. The priests by authority of the new nation, elected John Carroll as the first American bishop on May 18, 1789.

Immaterial of the sacrifice and the gains made, anti-Catholicism simmered underneath the veneer of the new country, causing several historians and those living at the time to comment; 'if it seems a bit strange that a war against a Protestant King George III could be cast as a fight against Catholicism, this was the paradox. Describing the Quebec Act as the turning point, General Thomas Gage puzzled over how colonists had become convinced that Britain would eliminate their religious freedom. When they could not "be made to believe the contrary…the Flame [of rebellion] blazed out in all Parts." Ambrose Serle, who served as secretary to Admiral Lord Richard Howe from 1776 to 1778, reported to his superiors that "at Boston the war is very much a religious war." Not surprisingly, some Britons over the years have chafed over the idea that the revolution was about lofty concepts of freedom.

In 1912, the English Cardinal Gasquet flatly declared that "the American Revolution was not a movement for civil and religious liberty; its principal cause was the bigoted rage of the American Puritan and Presbyterian ministers at the concession of full religious liberty and equality to Catholics of French Canada. " Yes, he noted, people were upset by taxation but that could have been resolved if not for the "Puritan firebrands and the bigotry of the people." [29]

---

29   www.catholichistory.net/Spotlights/SpotlightFounding.htm

QUESTIONS

1. What background behind the passing of the Quebec Act gave rise to the added furor of the colonists?
2. What gave reason for France and Spain to supply aid to the American Revolution?
3. What caused Catholics to become so assimilated into the prevailing Protestant culture and what were their reasons for justification?
4. What is the real value of the First Amendment?
5. What are the main reasons for the War of Independence from the Catholic point of view not in the school history books?

Chronological History of Religious Influence in the New World and Europe

1700-1800

* 1713: Encyclical Unigenitus condemns Jansenism.
* 1715: Clement XI rules against the Jesuits in the Chinese Rites controversy. Reversed by Pius XII in 1939
* 1721: Kangxi Emperor bans Christian missions in China.
* April 28, 1738: Pope Clement XII publishes the Bull *In Eminenti* forbidding Catholics from joining, aiding, socializing or otherwise directly or indirectly helping the organizations of Freemasonry and Freemasons under pain of excommunication. Membership to any secret society would also incur the penalty of excommunication.

* 1738: Grey Nuns founded.
* 1740–1758: Pope Benedict XIV, appointed first women as professors to Papal Universities in Bologna, reformed canonization procedures, intellectual open to all sciences;
* 1769: Passionist religious institute granted full rights by Clement XIV.
* 1769: Junípero Serra establishes Mission San Diego de Alcalá, the first of the Spanish missions in California
* 1773: Suppression of the Jesuits by Clement XIV, already excluded from many states. Only in the Russian Empire are they able to remain.
* 1789: John Carroll becomes the Bishop of Baltimore, the first bishop in the United States.
* 1793: French Revolution institutes anti-clerical measures.
* 1798: Pope Pius VI taken prisoner by the armies of Napoleon I, dies in captivity in France

Chapter Eight:
The Missions and Catholic Education
1600-1860

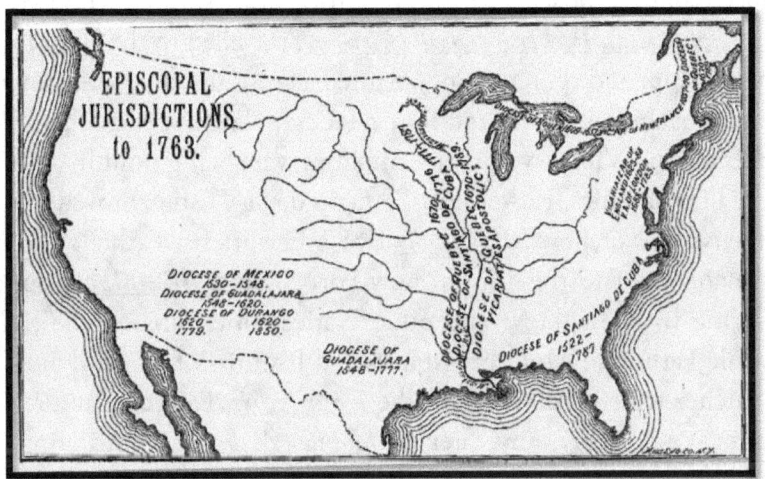

There is a bigoted and skewered in the historical representation which distorts and invalidates the major contributions the early Spanish and French missionaries established in North America to further not only the Catholic faith, but Catholic education as well. This same perception and discrimination also portrayed these brothers and priests with the same pitiless ferocity one associates with the conquerors of Spain and France over the southern and western regions of the continent. The preconception detracts the vitality of mission life which as its purpose became very much of a self-sustaining village well protected within its enclave. The objective was and is to work within the strengths of each tribe, retaining only religious instruction, the Mass and the Holy Sacraments.

Of the French Colonial Period, the territory under Jesuit missions contained what is now the States of Missouri, _Arkansas_, _Louisiana_, _Mississippi_, and Alabama, with the Tamarois foundation near Cahokia in _Illinois._ During 1673, the _Jesuit_ Marquette explored as far down the Mississippi to the villages in the Arkansas, later known as Quapaw, which is situated at the mouth of the river of the same name. This was the earliest map of the region specifying the position of the various tribes. By 1682, the Recollect _Franciscan Father Zenobius Membré_, travelled to the end of the Mississippi and on returning, planted a cross among the Arkansas, and preaching to them and to the Taensa, Natches, end others farther down. While two other seminaries were being built in among the Illinois tribes, Father Jean-François de St-Cosme; moved to the Taensa in Natchez, _Mississippi._ Two other priests, Father Antoine Davion went to the Tonica, now Fort Adams, _Mississippi_ also laboring with the _Yazoo_ and other Native Americans on the river, while Father de Montigny transferred his mission to lend aid for Natchez tribe. 1700 brought the _Jesuit father_, Paul du Ru, first to Biloxi, _Mississippi_, and later to _Mobile_, _Alabama_, ministering to the small tribes gathered about the French post, including a band of fugitive Apalachee from the revived Florida mission. _Jesuit_, Father Joseph de Limoges, followed, coming from _Canada_, planted a mission among the Huma and Bayagula, Choctaw bands about the mouth of the Red River, Louisiana.

1702 brought bloodshed, Father Nicholas Foucault of the Seminarists, was _murdered along_ with three companions, by the Koroa of Upper Mississippi. He was travelling to Mobile Their remains were found and _interred_ by Father Davion. 1706, Father St-Cosme, _murdered_ by the Shetimasha, near the mouth of the Mississippi, while asleep in a night camp.

By the threats coming from the Chickasaw in the name of English interest, the Tonica station was becoming in abandoned in 1708. At this point, for a time, the southern missions were languishing, the Indians themselves, indifferent and turning hostile to _Christianity_ When Father Charlevoix made his tour in 1721, he found only Father Juif, among the _Yazoo_. From his report, the Louisiana Company, gave permission to the _Jesuits_ to undertake all the Indian work, while the French posts and settlements were assigned to other _priests_. It would take another five years before the Arkansas would be restored under the tutelage of Father Paul du Poisson. It had been vacant since 1702. While Father Alexis de Guyenne went to the Alibamon, a tribe of the Creek nation, above Mobile, Father Mathurin le Petit began his work among the Choctaw in southern Mississippi. A year later, due to the efforts of the Jesuits, the French king gave the Ursuline sisters permission to settle in New Orleans where they opened the first convent in the United States, also building a hospital, an orphanage, and a school for girls. The next year found the _Jesuit father_, _Michel Baudouin_, undertaking a mission to the warring Chickasaw.

28 November, 1729 brought war with the Natchez over the arbitrary demands of the French commandeer. The massacre involved the whole French garrison, the first victim; Father du Poisson, who, on his way to a dying man, was struck down, his head decapitated. Father Souel was killed on 11 December by the _Yazoo_, who then turned upon the French garrison in their county. On New Year's Day 1730, the _Jesuit Father Doutreleau_ was fired upon by the Yazoo while saying _Mass_ on shore. He escaped, though badly wounded. Also in the same year, a newly arrived Seminarist, Father Gaston was killed at the Tamarois (Cahokia) mission. This _war_ involved the whole of the lower Mississippi spanning into 1736 which ended in the extinction of the Natchez as a people. Though part of the surviving Natchez fled to the Chickasaw in 1730, the war in 1736, caused a French expedition to be massacred, their

Jesuit chaplain, Father Antoninus Senat, burnt at the stake, and the last of Natchez killed.

Though the expulsion of the Jesuits in 1764 brought the Louisiana Mission to a close, prior, for eighteen years Father Baudouin continued with the Choctaw until 1757, when his place was filled by Father Nicholas le Febvre, on Fr. Baudouin's appointment as vicar-general. Their considerable faith carries forth despite the dictates or perhaps because of the secular world's demands for theft of lands and its people.

The Dakota, also called the Sioux, commanded territory which covered from the *Wisconsin* border to the foot of the Rocky Mountains. Within these vast lands, the Jesuits were unable to set up missions until 1837 when under Father Augustin Ravoux one was established among the Eastern Sioux in Minnesota. In 1848 the noted *Jesuit* missionary *Father de Smet* first preached to those west of the Missouri having previously founded the Flathead mission in Montana.in 1840. By 1847 the Osage mission in *Oklahoma had been created* by the *Jesuit Fathers* Schoenmaker and Bax also the Kiowa and Quapaw missions for the immigrant Choctaw, *Potawatomi*, and Miami. Others were established for the Winnebago in Nebraska and in North Dakota for the Mandan. Missions still in operation as well as throughout, Wyoming, Colorado and South Dakota.

Until the later part of the 1830's, Texas as a Spanish colony was part of Mexico, and ruled in missionary affairs from *Querétaro* and *Zacatecas*, instead of from *Havana*, as was Florida. Owing to the great expanse of land, in comparison, four times the size of New England, contained hundreds of bands –speaking a variety of languages and dialects. Under the guide of Franciscan missionaries, the first was Father Andres de Olmos, in 1544. For the next century and a half, though missions were expanding, there were continual land disputes between the kings of France and Spain and the various Native Americans against both and each other.

Two years after the French commandeer La Salle had built a fort on the banks of on Matagorda Bay in 1685, he departed leaving behind a small garrison of twenty including the Recollect missionaries, Fathers _Zenobius Membré_ and Maximus Le Clercq, and the Sulpician Father Chefdeville. A few months later, a Spanish expedition force arrived to dispossess the French, found only blackened ruins and unburied bones. All but two of the men had been killed by Indians, among whom the _chalices_ and Breviaries of the _murdered priests_ were afterwards recovered.

1690 realized a company of _Spanish Franciscans_ from the Querétaro College, headed by Father Damian Mazanet, established a mission among the Hasinai (Asinais, Cenis), in north-east _Texas._ In 1699 the _Franciscans_ of the _Zacatecas_ College began a series of missions along the south bank of the Rio Grande, to which they gathered in a number of Indians of the Pakawá group in southern _Texas_. These were kept up until 1718, when the chief mission was transferred to San Antonio in _Texas_.

To restore the Texas missions in 1715 the two colleges combined, under the venerable founder of the _Zacatecas_ College, _Father Antonio Margil_. The Hasinai mission (San Francisco) was restored and another, La Purísima, which had been established among the Hainai (Aynais) in the neighborhood of the present Nacogdoches. Another (N. S. de Guadalupe) was founded by _Margil_ himself among the Nacogdoches band of the Caddo in 1716, and others in 1717 among the Ais (N. S. de Dolores) and Adai or Adayes (San Miguel de Linares), the last being within the limits of _Louisiana_. In 1719, _war_ having been declared between _France_ and _Spain_, a French expedition under St-Denis plundered the mission at the Adai. In consequence the missions were abandoned until peace was declared two years later.

In 1718 the mission of _San Francisco_ Solano was transferred to San Antonio de Valero. Other missions were established in the vicinity, making a total of four in 1731, including San Antonio de Padua, the celebrated Alamo. In 1722 the mission of Guadalupe was established at *Bahia*, on Lavaca (Matagorda) Bay among the Karankawa. Nine years later it was moved to the Guadalupe River. In 1752 the Candelaria mission was attacked by the Coco, a Karankawa band, and Father José Ganzabal killed. In 1757 the mission of San Sabá was established by Father Alonso Terreros for the conversion of the wild and nomadic Lipan *Apache*, but they refused and in the following year destroyed the mission, killing Father Terreros and two other *priests*. Another Lipan mission was attempted in 1761, but was broken up by the Comanche in 1769. It was at this period in the history of *Texas* missions, with an Indian population of about 15,000 had reached their highest point. For the use of the San Antonio missions, Father Bartolomé García published his religious manual in 1760, which remains almost the only linguistic monument of the Pakawá tribes of central *Texas*. Though hampered by the *Spanish* authorities on a continual basis, the missions continued to stand, when in 1812, they were suppressed by the revolutionary Mexican government, and the Indians by necessity, scattered.

With the founding of Santa Fe in 1609, originally known as the Royal City of the Holy Faith of Saint Francis, she became the future headquarters for the future missions in New Mexico, by 1625 there were a total of 43 missions in New Mexico and 34,000 Christian Indians The Jesuit priest, Fr. Eusebio Francisco Kino, labored in the Upper Pima country, which is now the Mexican state of Sonora and southern Arizona. He has been referred to as "the most picturesque missionary pioneer of all North America explorer, astronomer, cartographer, mission builder, ranchman, cattle king, and defender of the frontier." His maps were the most accurate of the time, winning fame even in in Europe.

His mission of San Xavier del Bac, not far from what is now Tucson, Arizona, is a national monument, while still the parish church for the Pima Indians. It is the considered the finest example of Spanish Renaissance architecture in the United States. Throughout the thousands of miles he traversed, Father Kino kept and recorded volumes of journals which are housed in the Huntington Library in San Marino, California. Fr. Kino died on March 15, 1711, in poverty, as he had lived. But while he was grateful for winning the faith of the Pima Indians for Jesus Christ, he regretted he was unable to achieve the faith for the Apache. He is venerated as a great American pioneer.

In 1793 the Spanish crown withdrew its support and by 1824 the New Mexican Government suppressed the main mission of San Jos de Aguayo. The Franciscans were made to depart and passing of years the mission was neglected. (San Jos, which had earned the name Queen of the Missions, began to be restored to its former beauty in 1912 when the archdiocese of San Antonio began a restoration program. In 1941 arrangements began whereby it was named a National Historic Site.)

The Spanish built their missions not simply as churches for worshipers but to become self-sufficient communities with farms, cattle and ranches, and homes for Indians who worked at the mission also homes for teachers, nurses, and guards. They built hospitals, schools, and guard posts as protection from Apache and Comanche Indians. [30]

---

30   www.newadvent.org

Father Junipero Serra 1713-1784

Of the many strengths inherent within the Catholic Church, Her method of organization builds the sturdy foundation for the establishment for the parochial school system. This is what gave Fr. Junipero Serra, who is considered the great missionary of California, the ability to institute and construct the first of nine missions in California. Those who came after, established twelve more; San Diego, Carmel, San Gabriel, Santa Clara, San Luis Obispo, Ventura, Capistrano, San Francisco, to name a few. Though he began this journey of missionary work at the age of fifty-six, he and his order of Franciscans as the viceroy of Peru wrote to King Philip II: "They are the ones who preach the doctrine with the greatest care and example, and the least avarice." And in Father Serra's own words; "I have wanted to carry the Gospel teachings to those who have never heard of God and the kingdom He has prepared for them."

His felt his task entailed far more than bringing lost sheep into the fold, as with the Jesuits, Father Serra wanted to ensure each mission was self-sustaining by teaching all, the development of farmland for sowing and harvesting, the trades of construction, winepresses, mills, forges, and slaughterhouses. With his love for Christ and God and with no weapon, only his crucifix, Father

Serra carried out vocation until his death at the Carmel Mission on 28 August, 1784. Father Serra was seventy-one, being one of the last pioneers for the Spanish extension of the United States.

As parishes expanded, so to did the coverage of the areas under the diocese. To provide other examples than those already stated; the first bishop of the Cincinnati diocese the Dominican Father Edward Fenwick, which included in the 1820's, Ohio, Michigan and the Northwest Territory, established the Athenaeum Seminary which is known as Mount Saint Mary's Seminary of the West.

* In 1792 the Poor Clares came from France to open a monastery at Frederick, Maryland. In 1801 they opened an academy in Georgetown, which later was taken charge of by the Pious Ladies, the religious order founded in the United States in 1799. This society later became part of the Visitation Order.
* In 1824 in Florissant, Missouri as the Jesuits were opening a school for Indian boys the Ladies of the Sacred Heart opened one for Indian girls there.
* When Father Sorin and six lay brothers of the Congregation of the Holy Cross arrived to northern Indiana in 1841, they founded the college which they dedicated to Our Lady, we know it as Notre Dame du Lac.
* In 1842, in New Orleans, Bishop Blanc founded the Sisters of the Holy Family to take care of black people, especially orphans and the aged.
* In 1866 the Second Plenary Council of Baltimore met, with the bishops urging priests "as far as they can to consecrate their thoughts, their time and themselves, wholly and entirely if possible, to the service of the colored people."

The advent of the Catholic school system began in the face of bigotry, prejudice and laws designed to eradicate the Catholic from the soil of America. In spite of the decades of sanctions, the education of young Catholics in their faith and knowledge continued. As each mission, village and town was founded, there were also a priests and nuns to build the churches and schools. From the original thirteen colonies to the great expanse throughout the west, Catholicism left their indelible mark, and the majority of those schools and colleges are still flourishing.

QUESTIONS

1. What impact did the missions attain?
2. What was the mission's purpose?
3. What gave courage to the martyrs?
4. Why, in other history books were the missionaries portrayed with the same ferocity of dominance as the conquerors themselves?
5. Write a short journal from the point of view as a missionary

The missionary martyrs

Lest they be forgotten, this list is provided to show the number of missionaries who gave their lives for Christ. Their untimely death is in direct connexion with their work and gives credence that even before the establishment of the republic the soil of the

United States was *baptized* in the blood of *Catholic* missionaries from ocean to ocean.

* **1542.** *Juan de Padilla*, *Franciscan*, killed in Kansas (?).
* **1542.** Escalona, Brother Luis de, *Franciscan*, killed by Pecos, *New Mexico*.
* **1542.** La Cruz, Juan de, *Franciscan*, killed by Tigua, *New Mexico*.
* **1549.** *Luis Cancer*, *Dominican*, killed by Calusa, Florida.
* **1549.** Tolosa, Diego de, *Dominican*, killed by Calusa, Florida.
* **1549.** Fuentes, Brother, killed by Calusa, Florida.
* **1566.** Martínez, Pedro, *Jesuit*, killed by Yamasee, Georgia.
* **1569(?).** Báez, Brother Dom. Agustín, *Jesuit*, died of fever, with Yamasee, Florida.
* **1571.** Segura, Juan Bautista — Quiros, Luis de — Gómez, Brother Gabriel (novice) — Zerallos, Brother Sancho de (novice) — Solis, Brother — *Méndez*, Brother — Redondo, Brother — Linares, Brother — *Jesuits*, killed by Powhatan, Virginia.
* **1581.** López, Francisco, *Franciscan*, killed at Tigua, *New Mexico*.
* **1581.** Santa María, Juan de — Rodríguez (or Ruiz), Brother Agustín — *Franciscans*, killed at Tigera, *New Mexico*.
* **1597.** Corpa, Pedro de Rodríguez, Blas Auñon, Miguel de Velasco, Francisco de Badajóz, Brother Antonio — *Franciscans*, killed by Yamasee, *Georgia* and Florida.
* **1613.** Du Thet, Brother Gilbert, *Jesuit*, killed by the English, Maine.
* **1631.** Miranda de Avila, Pedro, *Franciscan*, killed by Taos, *New Mexico*.

* **1632.** Letrado, Francisco — Arvide, Martin de — _Franciscans_, killed by "Zipias", _New Mexico_.
* **1633.** Porras, Francisco, _Franciscan_, poisoned by Hopi, Arizona.
* **1642.** _René Goupil_ (novice), _Jesuit_, killed by Mohawks, New York.
* **1644.** _Joseph Bressani_, _Jesuit_, tortured by Mohawks, but rescued, New York.
* **1646.** Jogues, Isaac, _Jesuit_, killed by Mohawks, New York.
* **1653.** _Joseph Poncet_, _Jesuit_, tortured by Mohawks, but rescued, New York.
* **1657.** Eight _Franciscans_ drowned, _en route_ Florida missions to Havana.
* **1661.** Menard, René, _Jesuit_, lost, supposed killed by _Sioux_, _Wisconsin_.
* **1675.** "Several missionaries", _Franciscans_ (record incomplete), killed by Pueblos, _New Mexico_.
* **1675.** Marquette, Jacques, _Jesuit_, died in woods, Michigan.
* **1680.** La Ribourde, Gabriel de, Recollect, killed by Kickapoos, Illinois.
* **1680.** Twenty-two _Franciscans_ killed in general massacre by revolted Pueblos, _New Mexico_, and Arizona, viz.:
* Talaban, Juan, _Santo Domingo_ Pueblo, _New Mexico_.
* Lorenzana, Francisco Antonio de, _Santo Domingo_ Pueblo, _New Mexico_.
* Montes de Oca, (Juan?) José de, _Santo Domingo_ Pueblo, _New Mexico_.
* Pio, Juan Bautista de, Tesuque Pueblo, _New Mexico_.
* Torres, Tomas, Nambe Pueblo, _New Mexico_.
* Luis de Morales, San Ildefonso Pueblo, _New Mexico_.

* Pro, Antonio Sánchez* de, San Ildefonso Pueblo, <u>New Mexico</u>.
* Baeza, Luis de, San Ildefonso Pueblo, <u>New Mexico</u>.
* Rendon, Matias de, Picuris Pueblo, <u>New Mexico</u>.
* Mora, Antonio, <u>Taos Pueblo</u>, <u>New Mexico</u>.
* Pedrosa, Juan de, <u>Taos Pueblo</u>, <u>New Mexico</u>.
* Maldonado, Lucas, Acoma Pueblo, <u>New Mexico</u>.
* Bal, Juan de, Alona (Zuñi) Pueblo, <u>New Mexico</u>.
* Figueras, José de, Hopi Pueblos, Arizona.
* Trujillo, José Hopi Pueblos, Arizona.
* Espeleta, José de, Hopi Pueblos, Arizona.
* Santa María, Agustín de, Hopi Pueblos, Arizona.
* Bernal, Juan *(custos)*, Galisteo (Tano) Pueblo, <u>New Mexico</u>.
* Vera, Juan Domingo de, Galisteo (Tano) Pueblo, <u>New Mexico</u>.
* Velasco, Francisco (Fernando?), de, Pecos Pueblo, <u>New Mexico</u>.
* Tinoco, Manuel, San Marcos Pueblo, <u>New Mexico</u>.
* Jesus, Simon (Juan?) de, Jemes Pueblo, <u>New Mexico</u>.
* **1683.** *(circa)* Beltran, Manuel, <u>Franciscan</u>, killed by Tanos (?), <u>New Mexico</u>.
* **1687.** <u>Zenobius Membré</u>, Recollect — Le Clercq, Maximus, Recollect, Chefdeville, ____, Sulpician — killed by Karankawa (?), <u>Texas</u>.
* **1696.** ____, ____, <u>Franciscan</u>, by Ais (?) (Tororo), killed Florida.
* **1696.** Arbizu, José de, <u>Franciscan</u>, killed by Taos, <u>New Mexico</u>.
* **1696.** Carbonel, Antonio, <u>Franciscan</u>, killed by Taos, <u>New Mexico</u>.

* **1696.** Corvera, Francisco — Moreno, Antonio — _Franciscans_, killed by Tehua, _New Mexico_.
* **1696.** Casañes, Francisco, _Franciscan_, killed by Jemes, _New Mexico_.
* **1702.** Foucault, Nicholas, Sem. For. Missions, killed, by Koroa, Mississippi.
* **1704.** Parga, Juan de — Mendoza, Manuel de — Delgado, Marcos — Miranda, Angel — _Franciscans_, tortured and killed by English and Indian allies, Florida.
* **1706.** Delhalle, Nicholas, B.C., Recollect (_parish priest_, Detroit), killed by Ottawa, Michigan.
* **1706.** St-Cosme, Jean-François de, Sem. For. Missions, killed by Shetimasha, Louisiana.
* **1708.** _Jacques Gravier_, _Jesuit_, died of wound inflicted by Illinois (1705), Illinois.
* **1715.** (_circa_) Vatier, Léonard, Recollect, killed by Foxes, _Wisconsin_.
* **1718.** Mantesdoca (Mantes de Oca), Brother Luis de, _Franciscan_, killed in prairie fire, _Texas_.
* **1720.** (_circa_) Mingües, Juan, _Franciscan_, killed in massacre by Missouri, Missouri (?).
* **1721.** Pita, Brother José, _Franciscan_, killed in massacre by Lipan, _Texas_.
* **1724.** _Sebastien Rasle_ (Rasles, Râle), _Jesuit_, killed by English and Indian allies, Maine.
* **1729.** du Poisson, Paul, _Jesuit_, killed by Natches, Mississippi.
* **1729.** Souel, Jean, _Jesuit_, killed by _Yazoo_, Mississippi.
* **1730.** Gaston, ____, Sem. For. Missions, killed by Illinois, Illinois.
* **1736.** Senat, Antoninus, _Jesuit_, tortured and burned with whole party by Chickasaw, Mississippi.

* **1736.** Aulneau (Arnaud), Jean-Pierre, *Jesuit*, killed with twenty others in massacre by *Sioux*, on Massacre Island, Lake of Woods, about two miles beyond the Minnesota-Canada line.
* **1752.** Ganzabal, José Francisco, *Franciscan*, held by Coco (Karankawa), *Texas*.
* **1758.** (*circa*) Silva, –, *Franciscan*, killed by mission Indians, *Texas*.
* **1758.** Terreros, Alonso G. de — Santiesteban, José — *Franciscans* killed in massacre at San Sabá, by mission Indians, *Texas*.
* **1775.** Jayme, Luis, *Franciscan*, killed by Diegueño, *California*.
* **1780.** Díaz, Juan — Morena, Matias — Garces, Francisco — Barraneche, Juan — *Franciscans*, killed by Yuma, *California*.
* **1812.** Quintana, Andrés, *Franciscan*, killed by Mission Indians, *California*.
* **1833.** Díaz, ____, killed by Caddo (?), *Texas*. [31]

---

31 www.newadvent.org

Chapter Nine:
Archbishop Carroll and Saint Mother Seton

CARROLL, *John*, *R. C.* archbishop, born in Upper Marlborough, Maryland, in 1735; died in Georgetown, District of Columbia, in 1817. He was descended from the first family of Carrolls, whose representatives immigrated to Maryland about 1689, and whose members became possessed of vast landed estates in that province prior to the revolution. He was a cousin of Charles Carroll of Carrollton, and sympathized with him in his patriotic resistance to the British crown.

---

32   See more at: http://cardinalsblog.adw.org/2012/06/our-first-president-our-first--bishop-and-our-first-freedom/#sthash.XktPlz8Z.dpuf

What became troubling in America with its hard won freedoms was now, instead of maintaining consistent and constant with their Holy Faith, Catholic behavior, in wanting to become assimilated into the new country began to adopt a way of life that began to ignore and downplayed the very points of Catholic doctrine which Protestantism attacked. Several closed their eyes to the evil of this heresy and its mentality perhaps as a need to survive within the societal dictates and though this attitude may be explained away by the natural desire to achieve social and economic success, nonetheless it became a shameless attitude with regard to the glory of God and the doctrine that the Catholic Church as the only true religion, as well as dishonoring those whose blood fought and then spilled defending Catholicism. With this attitude continuing and intensifying, it generated a fellowship of sorts with Protestant beliefs and as such an errant Ecumenism was established within the American Catholic character. Where the doctrinal opposition between the two religions was becoming undervalued, what became the more important goal was the seeming emotional satisfaction of being accepted as Catholics in a predominant and Protestant society. The view was indeed overestimated. A disturbing seduction into our Catholic character was beginning to form and a little over a century later, Pope Leo XIII saw the cause and aptly named the sin, Americanism.[33]

Coupled in this vortex of melding and attempting to remain distinct, somewhat, was of course the doctrine; The Age of Reason. The thinking as well as the concept of life was directed in the cause of rationality, the concept of enlightenment and the great 'god' man's reason. The creation of the idea that revelation was no longer the province of God, but man's intellect away from the source of the ultimate truth. It was reasoned man was no longer bound from learning that the ultimate only could come from God, through

---

[33] Let None Dare Call it Liberty: The Catholic Church in Colonial America, Marian T. Horvat, Ph.D.

the intellect which was defined as the ability to form and operate upon concepts in abstraction, narrowing information to its bare content, without emotion. The viewpoint of rationality enclosed the theory of an ordered inference and comprehension leading to an understanding and hence the logical explanation. The 'prior dogmas of miracles, prophecy and religious rites were treated not only as unscientific in view of deductive reason, they smacked of superstitious beliefs better left to the uneducated

The result, society and man were now free to postulate his own theories of existence and his ideas about earth and its relation to the sun, though contemptuous of religion, most especially the Catholic Church, this 'age of reason' negated the Church's stance of the pursuit of knowledge by the gifts of intellect from God to man which is born in reason, yet governed and grounded in faith. As stated in Psalm 19:1-2 and Corinthians 3:19a; "The heavens declare the glory of God; the skies proclaim the work of his hands. Day after day they pour forth speech; night after night they display knowledge. The glory of God is clearly revealed in the works of God's hands. He alone is the giver of wisdom and knowledge. In deviating from the Bible, God's Word, as absolute truth, man has formulated all kinds of theories to explain his world "For the wisdom of this world is foolishness in God's sight."[34]

The components involved may appear innocuous, yet at the time, a very real distinction of values inherent in the Catholic faith, juxtaposed alongside the new hard won freedoms in America gave cause for the slow setting aside of values. There is a great and delicate responsibility inherent with freedom, for it is not the throwing aside of God in the name of manmade laws and rights, but rather the more important necessity of acknowledging the laws of God for the commitment to those very freedoms., which is in greater jeopardy in the present day.

---

34   www.allabouthistory.org/**age-of-reason**.htm

Yet within all the gains, America was expanding her boundaries with the seeds of ownership by rights which subsequently engendered the industrial revolution in the very near future, as was Europe. Though within all the burgeoning, American Catholics were keenly aware that their spiritual direction was under still auspices from London. To counteract an already suspicious climate for Catholic religious freedom, it was vital in this matter for a complete break from England. For which Father Carroll appealed to Rome, explaining how essential a native born American priest to govern spiritual matters and church doctrine was of the utmost importance. In this request, Pope Pius VII, relayed to the papal nuncio at Paris who consulting with Dr. Franklin, at the latter's request, Father Carroll was appointed superior of the clergy of the United States in 1784.

Five years after the ratification of the Constitution, the bishopric of Baltimore was established on a second petition from the clergy, and, Dr. Carroll being their choice for bishop, was consecrated in England in 1790. As the only Roman Catholic diocese in the United States, Baltimore oversaw all the states and territories of the union. The first priority required the need to ascertain the number of parishes and also giving attention to the French settlements in the west, which prior had its dependence on the bishop of Quebec. The greatest want was the need of priests, which became supplied by the eradication of Catholicism during the French Revolution, many emigrated to the United States. The Sulpicians were able to provide aid and support for the Indians and the French in the northwest. From England arrived the Dominicans and a community of Carmelite nuns as well as another of the Poor Clares.

To ensure the education of American Catholics and the training for American priests, Bishop Carroll in 1788 laid the foundation for Georgetown College, it was completed in 1791though the majority of aid he received from his English friends. The theological seminary was connected which in 1792[35] (Link for Archbishop Carroll's Pastoral Letter to the United States) was merged in that of St. Mary's, Baltimore. Shortly after the establishing of St. John's College at Annapolis, he received the degree of L.L.D. On 7 November, 1791.

Though Bishop Carroll held the only synod of his twenty-five year episcopacy, the main concerns, which he expressed in his pastoral letter, dealt with the administration of the sacraments and the support of the Church and at that first and only meeting, nothing was legislated in the area of education, his principal objectives.

In the ensuing years prior to 1800, the extent of his diocese expanded and the consequences as such made the spreading of God's word more difficult. The situation required the choice of either dividing his see into several dioceses or appoint a coadjutor to assist.in the enormous extent of his diocese. Dr. Carroll solicited Pope Plus VII, and in response to this request, the Rev. Leonard Veale was appointed his coadjutor in 1800. Further on, the Pope also erected Baltimore into an archiepiscopal see in 1808, with four Episcopal sees as suffragans with Bishop Carroll now the Archbishop of the United States.

---

35 Taken from "The National Pastorals of the American Hierarchy", edited by Rev. Peter Guilday, Ph.D. and published by the National Catholic Welfare Council, 1923. Provided Courtesy of: Eternal Word Television Network
5817 Old Leeds Road Irondale, AL 35210

With his resolve to continue the building of Catholic schools, Archbishop Carroll also established with the aid Mrs. Seton the institution of the Sisters of Charity at Emmetsburg in 1803. By 1806 he laid the foundation of the present cathedral of Baltimore, which he was enabled to dedicate before his death and in conjunction with them, framed additional rules for the government of the growing church. In 1808 Mount St. Mary's College and Seminary in Emmetsburg. Carroll would likewise give his approval to the founding of visitation nuns, who in 1799, under the direction of Leonard Neale, his successor, would begin Visitation Academy in Georgetown. In 1805 Carroll would urge English Dominicans to begin a priory and college in Kentucky for the large number of Maryland Catholics migrating there. And in 1805, not feeling a need to inform Rome of his intentions, he not only transferred Georgetown College to the Jesuits, he, by an affiliation with the Russian Jesuits, who had been protected from suppression by Catherine the Great, Archbishop Carroll restored the former missions in Maryland and Pennsylvania back to the Jesuits.

The remainder of his life was devoted to the interests of his diocese, which now embraced Maryland, Virginia, and the southern states as far as the gulf and the Mississippi. Although not taking an active part in politics, Archbishop Carroll was an ardent federalist, and always voted with his party. His writings are mostly controversial. Among them are "An Address to the Roman Catholics of the United States of America," "A Concise View of the Principal Points of Controversy between the Protestant and Roman Churches," "A Review of the important Controversy between Dr. Carroll and the Rev. Messrs. Wharton and Hawkins," and "A Discourse on General Washington." [36]

---

[36] Edited Appletons Encyclopedia by _John Looby_, Copyright (c) 2001 VirtualologyTM

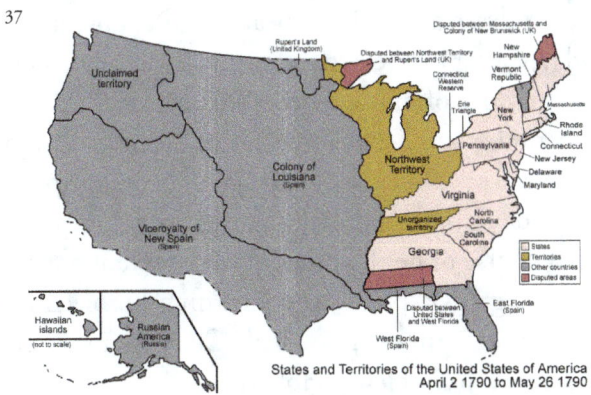

States and Territories of the United States of America
April 2 1790 to May 26 1790

St. Elizabeth Ann Seton
Foundress and First Superior of the Sisters of Charity in the United States
(b. August 28, 1774, New York City; d. Emmitsburg, Maryland, January 4, 1821)

Elizabeth Ann Bayley Seton, though born into an affluent Anglican family in New York, realized the wealth did not make her

---

37 States and Territories of the United States of America (April 2, 1790 to May 26, 1790) Images of Map of America 1790 bing.com/images

38 Copyright © 2013 St. Mary's Spiritual Center & Historic. All rights reserved. Site design by MPlank

mother's early death any easier to bear, nor the subsequent rejection of her and her sister by their step mother. By nature contemplative, she turned her love of music, poetry and nature as a ballast during the dark period when her beloved father separated from her step mother a few years after their marriage. To the introspective life, Elizabeth made full use of the first of the many journals she would write in the course of her life, the most consistent entries revolved around her religious aspirations concerning her need as a devout communicant at Trinity Episcopal Church and her spiritual director, the Rev. John Henry Hobart.

Within the upper social circles of the city, Elizabeth was part of the fashionable gatherings of many of the families and the attendance to their church. Much value and emphasis was placed around their faith. The Setons, being part of this world, Elizabeth's father Dr. Bayley would be well acquainted with the family. And so, on 25 January, 1794, Elizabeth married William Magee Seton. The year prior, William became a founding partner with his father in the import-export mercantile firm, the William Seton Company, which became the Seton, Maitland and Company in 1793, also conducting business as far afield as Italy with Filippo Filicchi (1763-1816), a renowned merchant of Livorno, Italy and a good friend.

Her husband's younger sister Rebecca, Elizabeth found a dear friend and what she referred to with affection, 'her soul friend and dearest confidante'. Together they, nursed the sick and dying among their family and friends, But most importantly the poorer neighbors in greater need of their assistance. To this end, The Society for the Relief of Poor Widows with Small Children (1797) was founded. Elizabeth was beginning to find her calling unaware of the irony that her life would soon be paved by the financial loss of the family business and the death of her husband in their travels to Italy for his health.

Death walked along with life more easily then, not that the bearing was any less than now, but parents buried their children as children buried their parents, well acquainted and trusting on God's strength to carry all home. Of the five born to Elizabeth and William, only two survived well into old age, Catherine and William Jr.

The events of France and Napoleon's quest as emperor, rippled its dire effects on American shipping companies, of which the Seton's import/export became a victim. Amidst losing ships from storms at sea, and others sinking by Napoleon's navy, the death of William's father and her own, (Dr. Bayley had established a "Health Establishment" on Staten Island for Irish immigrants quarantined because of the yellow-fever epidemic ravaging New York at that time- he himself contracted the disease from his patients. It is recorded that Elizabeth never left her beloved father's bedside[39]), foretold the beginning of the end. Adding to that both William and Elizabeth attempted to salvage the business and the welfare of both families living under one roof. At the time she was pregnant with their third child, but also enjoying the responsibility of here initial teaching duties for her daughters and William's younger sisters. Their financial situation would suffered the ignoble status of bankruptcy three years later. With the loss of the business, their house and possessions relinquished for the debts and the privileged life came to an abrupt demise. It was then her husband William began to show the signs of tuberculosis, the consequence perhaps of the extremity their life had come to. In a valiant and vain effort, the decision was made to voyage to the warmer climes of Italy in hopes to restore William's failing health. Elizabeth, William and their eldest, Anna Marie embarked for the port of Livorno in 1803. But the authorities, fearing the contagion of the yellow fever prevalent in New York at the time, the three were quarantined in a

---

39   17. Celeste, Marie, S.C. ed. Elizabeth Ann Seton: A Self-Portrait. Libertyville, Illinois: Franciscan Marytown Press, 1983.

cold stone lazaretto for a month. Though their friends the Filicchis did their utmost to provide comfort and relief, the conditions were primitive and two weeks after their release, William passed away in Pisa, 27 December, 1803. He was buried in the English cemetery in Livorno, leaving Elizabeth a widow at the age of twenty-nine with five young children to care for.

In mourning, Elizabeth began to have an inkling her Protestant faith perhaps contained cracks in its foundations caused by its own tear away, the grip to hold onto was crumbling. The Filicchis empathizing with her distress grief, introduced her to Catholicism and its constant solidity. At first to satisfy a sincere curiosity, she read the Memoreare and guided by Antonio and his wife Amabilia, Elizabeth Seton took her first steps of trying to understand Catholic practices. This interest soon gave way to wanting more depth of erudition regarding the Sacred Liturgy, the Real Presence of Christ in the Eucharist and the Church's direct unbroken link with Christ and the apostles. From this journey, Elizabeth wrote her Italian Journal[40], the long memoir for her sister-in-law Rebecca, in which she reveals the personal inner conflicts, heart-rending doubts and her conversion to becoming a Catholic in the ensuing year after her return. Thought out that winter and into the early spring of 1805 when Elizabeth and her daughter would return to New York, the Filicchis gave untold support, instruction and wise counsel of Catholic Doctrine. Coupled with all this, the necessary funds were provided for and Antonio also accompanied the pair back to America.

Though having left a firm Protestant, she arrived with the heart becoming fully into Catholicism. This was ill received with the society she had left, most especially with her husband's family. Their ire and hostility coupled on the death of her beloved sister-in-

---

40 Sisters of Charity, Federation of." New Catholic Encyclopedia. 2nd Edition. Farmington Hills, Michigan: The Gale Group/Thomson Learning, Inc., 2003. cf. Bechtle and Metz, p. 243

law Rebecca, caused great turmoil and anguish. The dire financial situation exuberated her religious strength as the sole parent of five children under the age of eight and the constant moving to cheaper and cheaper lodgings as the money dwindled away.

In these grim circumstances, Elizabeth prayed for discernment on God's will for her future, it was then she realized how her prism of faith would be bound with the Virgin Mary and her bounty as the world's Mother. The wrestle with doubts and fears in her search for truth, Elizabeth found resolve through the guidance the Rev. John Cheverus, the first bishop of Boston. The conflicts melted and Reverend Matthew O'Brien received Elizabeth's profession of the Catholic faith at Saint Peter's Church on Barclay Street in lower Manhattan on 14 March, 1805. She took her First Holy Communion two weeks later on the 25th by Bishop John Carroll who she considered to be her spiritual father and became confirmed the next year on Pentecost Sunday. She chose the name Mary as her confirmation name and realized how each of her three names had special significance in the mysteries of Salvation for her.

In consequence of the anti-Catholic prejudices of New York, Elizabeth's initial years as a Catholic were constantly marked by disappointments and failures in her need to provide for her family. Her attempts to secure teaching positions and the venture to open a boarding school for boys were all met blatant intolerance and discrimination. The Seton family itself fostered their own fears of contamination of Catholics by sequestering the younger brothers and sisters of William away from Elizabeth's influence. To no avail, Cecilia became a convert in 1806 and Harriet followed suit in 1809. It was during Cecilia's early struggles in the new found faith that Elizabeth wrote an instructive Spiritual Journal which offered wise counsel.

Amidst all the frustrations, bigotry and the constant worry for her children, Elizabeth remained steadfast in her faith. As a mother first and foremost, she examined all the alternatives for their future when by providence she met with Rev. William Dubourg, S.S. in 1806. Since 1797 he had desired a congregation of religious women to teach girls in Baltimore. With the concurrence with Bishop Carroll, Elizabeth was invited to Baltimore along with French priests belonging to the Society of Saint Sulpice, they would be assisting her in forming plans for the best interests of her own children and starting a school for the religious instruction of the young of that city.

The vision of the Sulpicians was for creating a sisterhood modeled on the Sisters of Charity in Paris and they, with energy recruited and enlisted candidates from the germinal community. Several ladies joined, but only Elizabeth took the vows of chastity and obedience in the lower chapel of Saint Mary's on 25 March, 1809. Archbishop Carroll gave her the title of Mother Seton. (Of this day, Mother Seton wrote: My object in pronouncing them is to embrace poverty, under whose roof I desire to live and die; chastity, so lovable and so beautiful, that I truly find all my happiness in cultivating it; and above all, obedience, the sure refuge and safeguard of my soul.) Two months later the sisters appeared together for the first time dressed alike, for Elizabeth had taken as their habit the black dress, cape and bonnet patterned after the widows' weeds of the women in Italy. Elizabeth spent one year as a school mistress in Baltimore.

During her tenure in Baltimore, Samuel Cooper, a convert, conceived of a plan to establish an institution for girl's Catholic education, services for the elderly, a department for enhancing and the training for job skills and a small manufactory to ease those oppressed by poverty, all of which to be contained in one area. He purchased 269 acres in Emmitsburg, Maryland for that purpose. For this endeavor, his thought was to have Elizabeth to direct the entire curriculum.

Though the beginning few years were fraught with poverty and fairly unsettling, Elizabeth kept her unfailing faith in God's Divine plan for herself and her sisters. The period of 1809 through 1820, brought ninety-eight candidates, of which eighty-six joined the new community and remained Sisters of Charity under Mother Seton.

By adapting the seventeenth century French Common Rules of the Daughters of Charity to the needs of the American Catholic Church, Elizabeth formed her sisters in the Vincentian spirit. Each year on 25 March they made vows of poverty, chastity, obedience and service to the poor.

To carry on their mission, Mother Seton and the Sisters of Charity intertwined Catholic social ministry with education in the faith and the religious values in all they undertook. In 1814, the sisters were sent to Philadelphia to open and manage the first Catholic orphan asylum, the year following saw the opening at Saint Mount Mary's for underway an infirmary and domestic services for the college and the seminary. By 1817, another orphanage was opened in New York City, Saint Joseph's, later renamed Saint Patrick's Orphan Asylum. From these burgeoning fruits of humble labor, Mother Seton and her Sisters of Charity carried on the firm knowledge of how much Christ is present in all of us. Her living legacy is seen by her firm commitment to God's wisdom and Will and the joyful knowledge of the living Eucharist All those under her care, the orphans, widows and poor families benefited not only from her value for the need of religious education, but how the multiple forms of poverty can caused untold stress and despair. She was able to see how inward oppression of poverty can burden those already without hope of escaping their fate. This empathy and understanding can best be relayed by Mother Seton own words in a letter to her friend Julia Sitgreaves Scott, 'For my part, I find so much contentment in this love (of God) that I am obliged to put on my consideration cap to find out how anyone can raise their eyes to the light of heaven and be insensible to it...

Faith lifts the staggering soul on one side, Hope supports it on the other. Experience says it must be, and love says- let it be. And so goes your friend thro' her passing career'. ... She goes on to say later: 'My soul is free and contented as it has been burthened and afflicted, for God has been so gracious to me as to remove every obstacle in my mind to the true Faith and given me strength to meet the difficulties and temptations I am externally tried with'.

On 4 January, 1821 Mother Seton passed away and in her last breathes extorted her sisters to "Be children of the Church, be children of the Church." With the extent of her vows as a Sister of Charity, in 1882, Archbishop Gibbons initiated her cause for canonization. In 1940 it was officially introduced to the Vatican, where the cause made steady progress. Blessed John XXIII declared Mother Seton venerable on 18 December, 1959, and also beatified her on 17 March, 1963. During the Holy Year of 1975, Pope Paul VI canonized Saint Elizabeth Ann Seton on 14 September. The Holy See accepted three miracle through her intercession the cures of Sister Gertrude Korzendorfer, D.C., (1872-1942), of Saint Louis, of cancer; a young child, Ann Theresa O'Neill, (b.1948), of Baltimore, from acute, lymphatic leukemia; and the miraculous recovery of Carl Kalin, (1902-1976), of New York, from a rare form of encephalitis.

Her writings are prolific and can be found in the Rare Books and Special Collections, Hesburgh Library, University of Notre Dame, Indiana, and in the Simon Bruté Collection of the Old Cathedral Library, Vincennes, Indiana and the archives at Saint Joseph's Provincial House, Daughters of Charity of Saint Vincent de Paul in Emmitsburg, Maryland. Her remains repose in the Basilica of Saint Elizabeth Ann Seton at Saint Joseph's Valley.

At the time of her death, the American Sisters of Charity, the first to be founded in the United States, had twenty houses spread throughout the country. There are now five independent communities of the Sisters of Charity and a sixth which merged with the French Daughters of Charity in 1850. The sisters now staff hospitals, child-care institutions, homes for the aged and handicapped and schools at all levels. The community is also found in South America, Italy and in various mission countries.

Mother Seton's Habit

QUESTIONS

1. Why did Archbishop want to maintain a distinct identity for American Catholics?
2. How did the Age of Reason affect Catholicism?
3. What were the contributions from Archbishop Carroll?

4. What causes created Saint Elizabeth's conversion to Catholicism and why did she refer to her Protestant religion as 'dear ashes'?
5. Why is Saint Elizabeth known as the founding Mother of parochial schools?
6. What are the legacies of Saint Elizabeth?

Chronological History of Religious Influence in the New World and Europe

1800-1900

* 1800–1823: *Pope Pius VII*
* July 16, 1802: French Concordat of 1801. The Catholic Church re-established in France.
* December 2, 1804: Napoleon crowns himself Emperor of the French in the Cathedral of *Notre Dame, Paris*, in the presence of Pope *Pius VII*.
* 1846: *Pope Pius IX* begins his reign. During his reign he asks that an anti-Catholic document written by Freemasons known as the *Alta Vendita* be distributed to alert Catholic officials of possible Masonic infiltration.
* 1847: The *Latin Patriarch of Jerusalem* resumes residence in Jerusalem.
* 1850: The *Archdiocese of Westminster* and twelve other dioceses are set up, re-establishing a Catholic hierarchy in the United Kingdom against intense political opposition.
* 1852: The First *Plenary Council of Baltimore* is held in the United States.
* 1854: *Dogma* of the *Immaculate Conception* by *Pope Pius IX*

* 1858: Apparitions in _Lourdes_.
* December 8, 1869: _Pope Pius IX_ opens the _First Ecumenical Council of the Vatican_
* July 18, 1870 – The Dogmatic Constitution of the Church of Christ from the fourth session of Vatican I, "Pastor Aeternus", issues the dogma of _papal infallibility_ among other issues before the fall of Rome in the _Franco-Prussian War_ causes it to end prematurely and brings an end to the _Papal States_. Controversy over several issues leads to the formation of the _Old Catholic Church_. This council was not formally closed until 1960 by Pope John XXIII in preparation for the Second Vatican Council.
* 1879: Encyclical _Aeterni Patris_, by Pope _Leo XIII_, prepares a revival of _Thomism_.
* May 15, 1891: Pope _Leo XIII_ issues encyclical _Rerum Novarum_ (translation: Of New Things).
* November 30, 1894: Pope Leo XIII publishes the _Encyclical Orientalium Dignitas_ (On the Churches of the East) safeguarding the importance and continuance of the Eastern traditions for the whole Church.
* 1897: _Thérèse of Lisieux_ dies.
* 1898 – Secondo Pia takes the first photographs of the _Shroud of Turin_.

Chapter Ten:
Anti-Catholic Riots in the Nineteenth Century

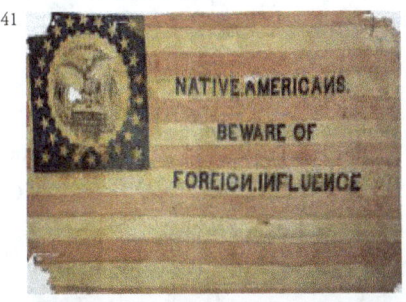

"Congress shall make no law respecting an establishment of religion or prohibiting the free exercise thereof." Such was and is the law, yet each state maintained and preserved their own right to regulate the question of religion and of a state Church. The elimination of penal codes against Catholics were slow and met with

---
41   *The Know-Nothing Party flag.*

a great deal of resistance. Cases in point come from a) not until 1833 that the union between *Church and State* in the Commonwealth of *Massachusetts* was dissolved, and *Catholics* were relieved from having to pay taxes for the support of the state (*Protestant*) Church; b) New Jersey retained its anti-Catholic Constitution until 1844, and c) only in 1877 did *New Hampshire* expunge from its Constitution the provision disqualifying *Catholics* from holding office in that state. As seen through the beginnings and throughout the nineteenth century, freedom of religion was in the Federal Constitution, it was barely accepted in theory, let alone conducted in practice. By the time of the War of 1812, the French Catholics were once again reviled which also reflected on American Catholics and in consequence, the somewhat submerged prejudice reasserted itself and began to gain momentum with the arrival of large numbers of Irish immigrants during 1817, the first of devastating potato famines in Ireland in the nineteenth century. To quote; "The foundation of a Catholic Church in Boston could only be surpassed by devoting a chamber in the Vatican to a Protestant Chapel" said William Tudor, writing in his "Letters on the Eastern States" (Boston, 1819) [42]

A subtle shift away from the dominant agricultural communities to the rising dominance of cities and their segregation of incoming immigrants. Though cultures will bind themselves within their own, it was the rise of tenements and the subsequent use of cheap labor for the lowest jobs, helped to foster what is termed at the 'Great Riot Year of the 1834'[43]. Of all the twenty-four riots that occurred from January through December, ten were instigated by Protestants against the Irish and Catholics, both of which were one and the same. The fear which was reviving itself in the 1820's, was not only the greater number of Catholics, but the more outspoken

---

42   www.newadvent.org

43   1834 The Great Riot Year, Carl E. Prince, University of Pennsylvania Press Society for Historians of the Early American Republic; *www.jstor.org/stable/3122502*

and authoritarian stance of the Papacy denouncing the modernism and liberalism in the United States. This was conceived as a serious threat of how much Catholics posed to Protestant America. Conspiracy rumors for an imminent Papal takeover ran the gamut, fueling the hatred already in place. One first example occurred in Boston when in 1825, the Irish population numbered about 5,000, anti-Irish gangs attack families and their property on Ann and Broad Streets. At the time Mayor Quincy posted six watchmen to maintain the peace. By 1832, he was petitioned to take steps to prohibit further violence. This was not an isolated occurrence, for the 1820's were pockmarked by such, which exposed the resentment of a growing alliance of individuals becoming known as The Nativists. It was their conviction that they were the 'Native Americans', disregarding in their view all those who were here long before their arrival, they considered themselves true Americans. This particular group and several prominent evangelical preachers, including Lyman Beecher, Reverend Henry Ward Beecher and Samuel Morse publish anti-Catholic pamphlets suggesting that the Irish are secret agents in a Popish plot to undermine Anglo-Saxon New England as they were convinced that Catholicism was a faith characterized by an authoritative religion which was completely incompatible with republicanism. Catholics were viewed as submissive and unquestioning followers, who therefore lacked the individuality and free thinking required of democratic citizens. Moreover, the Catholic immigrant, whose numbers were growing, kept their allegiance to a foreign ruler, and were seen as disloyal and to the many, even treasonous to the American ideals.

In July of 1827, the Ursuline Covent and School, which had outgrown their dwelling next to the Cathedral of Holy Cross on Franklin Street in Boston, was granted permission from Bishop Cheverus to build on what was known as Ploughed Hill later called Convent Hill or Mount Benedict in the town of Charlestown, which was separate from Boston, now known as Somerville. The young ladies attending the school, were mainly from the prominent Protestant families of the surrounding area. Of the forty-seven students in 1834, only six were Catholic.

American history books pay little heed to the causes of the numerous anti-Catholic riots of the nineteenth century. The reasons and contributing factors did not coincide with the value of how the country portrayed the founding of its beliefs and principles. The truth would present blots on her copybook, for then as now cheap labor was one of the governing forces for the economy. And when the Irish rioted against their working conditions in the canals and railroads gave further proof of how despicable the Irish Catholic immigrant was and how unfit he was to understand the concepts of liberty in a democratic society. This magnified the deeply held suspicions of Catholic ritual and life not only within the Church, but more so the religious life in the convent and seminary.

Prior to the burning of the Ursuline Convent, false rumors and accusations ran amuck. From the Mother Superior and Bishop Fenwick colluding to take over Boston, to young Protestant girls being held against their will and made to convert, as well as the fabricated reports of beatings, abortions, kidnappings and the stories of barbarities practiced on the nuns, of dying men cruelly treated and of immoralities which infested daily life. One young servant, Rebecca Theresa Reed was approached by a publisher shortly after her dismissal from the convent. Her 'book' titled "The Nun" created immediate alarms in Boston and Charlestown, she stated that she was 'lucky enough to escape from the miserable confines of such a malicious institution'.[44] Little proof was needed and from the 11th to the 14th of August, 1834 Protestant mobs attacked and ransacked the convent and then burned it to the ground. No-one was injured. Of the four arrests, all were acquitted and restitution, never materialized.

---

44 Burning of the Ursuline convent **Gregory Cronin**, *Colby College* 1986 Honors Thesis Colby College. American Studies Dept.

RUINS OF THE URSULINE CONVENT, AT CHARLESTOWN, MASSACHUSETTS.

To understand the very real hatred and absolute conviction of the American Protestant mindset, specifically through the years of 1834-35, against Catholicism, is to attempt to fathom the depth of how its religious and political differences were made to isolate and remove the 'Catholic Problem'. The Native American Movement believed their democratic country was the one and only true faith; all others, especially Popery, was the anti-Christ to its principles. Yes, all this, yet the actual animosity, then as now stemmed from the devastating economic depression of the late 1830s and early1840s. It was this economic insecurity and mechanization and burgeoning industrialism of many crafts and trades, which created the resentment on the part of the native-born labor population. 'They' were taking the worst and cheapest jobs, though the view was stealing work from the "native" Americans. In all neighborhoods in which they were allowed to settle, Irish immigrants formed their own community and social networks which centered on the church, the tavern, and the volunteer firehouse. The "nativists" especially in Kensington accused the Irish of isolating themselves from the larger society and being unwilling to assimilate and the very real fear these largely poor, unskilled Irish immigrants drove down wages by working for next to nothing stoked nativist antipathies. (The Irish often felt the same way about African Americans, their closest competitors for scarce jobs and housing, and Irish violence against blacks was common in the 19th century.)

The evidence pointed to a Catholic mob attacking an anti-Catholic Protestant meeting on 15 March, 1835. The resulting action came swift in the formal organization of the Native American Party. To further their cause by educating the public of the imminent dangers to the Republic, various newspapers were established between New York and Boston; "The Protestant", "The Protestant Vindicator", "The Downfall of Babylon".[45]

Throughout the decade prior to the Philadelphia Riots, (also referred as the Bible Riots), in May 1844, the "evils of Popery and the Irish labor riots" remained the focal argument for maintaining the separation of Church and State. So, when Bishop Kenrick made a request to the controllers of Philadelphia's public schools, in 1842, the precedent was set for the resulting riots. It began simply enough, in the 1840's students began the day reading the Protestant version of the Bible. The Bishop wrote a letter asking that Catholic children read the Douai and be excused from other religious teaching while attending public school. Permission was granted and the matter was closed. A year later, a rumor circulated that pushed a simmering tension into bloodshed. Mr. Hugh Clark, who was a school director in the Kensington district and a Catholic, was visiting a girl's school, where, as the allegations stated; he demanded the principal stop Bible reading in school. This version of the story claimed the principal refused and that she would rather lose her job than acquiesce. Mr. Clark refuted this version, asserting that several students had chosen to read a different version of the Bible, perhaps if confusion was the result then perhaps it would be better not read. This spurred the outrage with proved that Catholics were indeed the agents of the Pope and received the direct order to remove the Bible from schools., also

---

45   www.newadvent.org/cathen

misusing Bishop Kenrick's requests as further proof of the specific attacks against the Protestant Bible. But, following the riots, Archdiocesan Bishop Francis Patrick Kenrick abandoned his efforts to influence the public schools and instead laid the groundwork for the Catholic school system.

---

46   Bishop Francis Kenrick, en.wikipedia.org/wiki/File:KenrickFrancis

47   Engraving of the "Rioters in Kensington" from A Full and Complete Account of the Late Awful Riots in Philadelphia, Philadelphia: John B. Perry, 1844

St. Michael's Church on fire

Saint Augustine's Church on fire

FAroof of Irish instability for American liberty, the American Republican party, (the Protestant nativist group) on 3 May, 1844 held a meeting in a part of the Kensington District which was predominantly Irish Catholic laborers. The engineered scheme succeeded and the group was attacked, whereby they retreated. Three days later returning with reinforcements, they held their meeting in the nearby market using inflammatory speakers to denounce the Irish Catholics of the Kensington neighborhood and called for Americans to defend themselves from 'the bloody hand of the Pope'. On 7 May, the Nativists set fire to the Hibernia fire station, thirty homes were destroyed in the Kensington neighborhood and

---

48 www.en.wikipedia.org/wiki/philadelphia_nativist_riots

the market itself was also lost. A brief lull ensued by the belated arrival of the local state militia. They could do little to curb the riot and the following day, the mob returned in greater numbers, burning down Saint Michael's and the rectory, the Seminary of the Sisters of Charity, Saint Augustine's Church and also a nearby school which housed a collection of rare books. A statement from Bishop Kenrick ordered all churches to be closed the following Sunday to avoid further provocation and violence and the Mayor set up a force to protect Catholic Churches. All valuables were removed from the churches and hidden in homes for safekeeping. The report issued on 18 June, a *grand jury* blamed an imperfect response by law enforcement and the Irish Catholics for the riots, stating that the outbreak of violence was due to "the efforts of a portion of the community to exclude the Bible from the public schools" and the disruption of legitimate meetings by immigrants [Nativists said they were only responding to being attacked and were justified in their actions but were not responsible for the riots after May 6. The American Republican Party issued a statement blaming Mayor Scott, the sheriff, and the civil authorities for the riots. [49]. At the May's riots end, at least fourteen people were killed in the Kensington District, an estimated fifty people were injured and two hundred had fled their homes. The financial damage wrought $150,000, in today's terms, $3.76 million.

For the next eight weeks a festering stillness stayed quiet, each side eying the other for the next excuse for eruption. It came on 5 July when a Catholic priest's brother began stockpiling weapons in the cellar of Saint Philip de Neri Church in the neighborhood of Southwark. The response was immediate, thousands gathered outside demanding the surrender of all arms. The militia intervened, turning the crowd back, but the violence escalated on the seventh causing greater violence. The rioting lasted well into the night with the additional arrival of troops from other parts of Philadelphia.

---

49   www.en.wikpedia.org/wiki/philadelphia_nativist_riots

Though the Church remained untouched, the carnage left several more dead and wounded. As with the May riots, a grand jury once again blamed the Irish Catholics for the riots. More than two thousand Philadelphians signed an address praising the militia's use of "lawful force which unlawful force made necessary."

50

The outcome further entrenched the prejudice against the Irish and Catholics and the riots gained the national attention and its condemnation. Used as an issue in the <u>1844 U.S. Presidential election</u>, the <u>Democratic Party</u> denouncing the growing Native American Party and the <u>Whig Party</u>. Irrespective of the accusations from the Democrats, in Philadelphia, the Native American Party made a strong showing in the city's October election. From this there were fears the nativists would target New York City's Catholic churches. It was Archbishop <u>John Hughes</u> who organized defenders for the churches and told the mayor that if any churches were burned, "New York would be another Moscow."

---

50   (Library Company of Philadelphia)

Bishop John Hughes, circa 1861

An Gorta Mor: Irish Gaelic for The Great Hunger. During the 1845-1849 Ireland lost her great resource, the one third who survived, emigrated to America, for the two thirds left behind, a million starved to death. This massive influx became the rallying cry for the weakening Nativist Party to burgeon into a leading political force. In 1852 in New York City the Knownothing Party formally designed itself into a national organization and presence. The leaders gather all Native American groups under a single heading, the National Council of the United States of America. 'Its published ritual declared (Article II) the purpose of the organization to be "to protect every American citizen in the legal and proper exercise of all his civil and religious _rights_ and privileges; to resist the insidious policy of the _Church_ of _Rome_ and all other foreign influence against our republican institutions in all lawful ways; to place in all offices of _honour_, trust or profit in the

---

51 www.pahrc.net/index.php/anti-catholicism-jacksonian-philadelphia/huges-john--ca-1861

gift of the people or by appointment none but Native American Protestant citizens". Article III declared "that a member must be a native-born citizen, a Protestant either born of _Protestant_ parents or reared under _Protestant_ influence, and not united in marriage with a Roman Catholic. . .no member who has a _Roman Catholic_ wife shall be eligible to office in this order", etc. There were several degrees of membership as there were also state, district, and territorial councils, all of them subordinate to the National Council. The organization had the usual equipment of secret signs, grips, passwords, and the like. [52] Such were the dictates and demanded loyalty required and by its very language inciting mobs to do its bidding without any reasoned logic, criminal acts of violence went unchecked. Though their reign was brief politically, only the years from 1851-1855, the damage to Catholics, barely warrants a footnote. Yet the record is not obliterated, for the evidence is readily found provided ones digs.

In 1851 the hue and cry rallied against the building for the Sisters of Mercy under the direction of Mother Xavier Warde in _Providence_, R. I.. The cottage the Sisters was attacked at night, and the windows broken. During the day, the sisters were verbally assaulted and threatened continually with the destruction of their convent as well as the Bishop's house and other Catholic Churches. To avert the any disorder, the mayor sent a request for the sisters to remove themselves from Providence. They in turn appealed to the civil authorities for protection, to little avail, a fully armed group of the Knownothing party assembled for the attack. They were met by Bishop O'Reilly and a number of Irish Catholics guarding the convent stating all will be protected at all costs. In a rare move the mob dispersed.

In 1853, the _Archbishop Bedini_, the Apostolic Nuncio to the Court of _Brazil_, came to visit various cities in America. The alarm was considerable among the Knownothing Party and with each city hostile protests were conducted. _Boston_, _Baltimore_, _Wheeling_, St.

---

52 American Politics, Book I, pp. 57-9

Louis, and Cincinnati during solemn religious celebrations, scenes of disorder, and bloodshed took place, provoked by the Knownothing speakers both lay and _clerical_, as well as by the anti-Catholic press. There was the attempt in Cincinnati where a mob of 600 armed men carrying lighted torches and ropes, marched to the _cathedral_ intending to set it on fire and, as was believed, to hang the Nuncio. The encounter was met with police and the mob was dispersed, but not until after shots had been fired and several _persons_ wounded. Throughout 1854, assaults upon _Catholic_ churches escalated, St. Mary's in _Newark_, N. J., was invaded by a mob made up of Knownothings and Orangemen from _New York City_. The windows were broken, some of the statuary destroyed, and one unoffending bystander, an _Irish Catholic_, was shot and killed. In October of the same year, at Ellsworth, _Maine_, _Father John Bapst, S.J._, was dragged from the church, robbed of his watch and money, tarred and feathered, and ridden about the village on a rail.

On 4 July, at _Manchester_, N. H., St. Anne's church was attacked, its windows broken, its furniture destroyed and the _priest_ compelled leave. Houses of _Irish Catholics_ were attacked and families driven out, even the sick being dragged from their beds. In Bath, Maine, the mob broke into the church wrecking the altar, the _pulpit and_ setting fire to the building, it burned to ashes. In Dorchester, _Massachusetts_, a keg of gunpowder was placed under the floor of the _Catholic_ Church, it was fired at three o'clock in the morning and resulted in almost the total destruction of the building. In another _Catholic_ church, at Sidney, _Ohio_, was blown up with gunpowder. In Massillon, _Ohio_, another church was burned, and an attempt made to burn the _Ursuline_ Convent at _Galveston, Texas_. At Lawrence and at Chelsea, _Massachusetts_, the _Catholic_ churches were attacked by the Knownothings. St. Mary's church at Norwalk, Conn., was set on fire and later its cross was sawed off the spire. A fire was started in the church of Sts. Peter and Paul in _Brooklyn_, and the building was saved only by the interference of the police aided by the militia. St. Mary's Church at Saugerties, N. Y., were set on fire and nearly destroyed with the attempt to burn the church at _Palmyra_, N. Y. During the elections taking place in Louisville, Kentucky in 1855, the result of the Knownothing agitation caused rioting, bloodshed and the cathedral was invaded, so that the day, (5 August), became known as Bloody Monday. Later Bishop Spalding sent a letter to _Bishop Kenrick_ summing up the results of the day's proceedings, "We have just passed through a reign of terror surpassed only by the Philadelphia riots. Nearly one hundred poor _Irish_ have been butchered or burned and some twenty houses have been consumed in the flames. The City authorities, all Knownothings, looked calmly on and they are now endeavoring to lay the blame on the _Catholics_"[53]

As the gains increased in the legislatures, again hostile measures and bills were proposed against Catholics, more specially the Irish catholic immigrants. In some states there were proposition to authorize the visitations and inspections of convents and other religious institutions by state officials. In 1854 a bill in Massachusetts, known as the Nunneries Inspection Bill indeed passed. Under this an appointed committee could make a tour of inspection unannounced to _Catholic_ colleges and _convents_. Other states, in particular New York, _church property_ bills were proposed to destroy the title to _Catholic Church property. The name on the title was usually the bishop_, then there being no law for the incorporation of _Catholic_ churches by which such title might be securely held. Congress were making efforts to restrict the benefits of the Homestead Laws to only citizens of the _United States. Also an_ old-time proposal was debated to support the same laws by extending the period of residence to twenty-one years before a _person_ could be admitted to citizenship. Other _laws_ and ordinances were passed in _Massachusetts_ disbanding volunteer militia companies bearing the name of an _Irish_ patriot, peopled for the most part of _Catholic Irishmen_.

---

53   Life of Archbishop Spalding", by J.L. Spalding, p. 185

In article after article of the Knownothing owned newspapers, propounded by both their secular and religious, these measures were applauded and advocated to eradicate the 'Catholic Menace' from American liberty and principles. In the controversy involving Bishop Hughes and Senator Brooks over the New York Property Bill, it gained the whole country's attention validating the charges made against Catholics written in volumes of anti-Catholic pamphlets. In their book "Life of Lincoln", authors Nicolay and Hay state: "Essentially it was a revival of the extinct Native American faction based upon a jealousy of and discrimination against foreign born voters, desiring an extension of their period of naturalization and their exclusion from office; also based upon a certain hostility to the *Roman Catholic* religion." [54]

Also in Schouler, History of the United States, a non-Catholic historian, says: "They [the Knownothings] revived the bitter spirit of intolerance against the *Roman Catholic Church* such as ten years before had been shown in the riots of Charlestown and Philadelphia, by representing it as foreign, the handmaid of popular *ignorance* and bent on chaining Americans to the throne of the Vatican. . . . Catholic churches were assaulted every now and then by some crowd of Bible bigots helped on by the brawny friends of free fight inflamed by street preachers and the revelations of 'converted *Jesuits*' and 'escaped *nuns*' etc."[55] Bishop Spalding's wrote; "they were the depraved portion of our native population. It was not the American people who were seeking to make *war* on the *Church*, but merely a party of religious fanatics and unprincipled demagogues who as little represented the American people as did the mobs whom they incited to bloodshed and incendiarism. Their whole conduct was un-American and opposed to all the principles and traditions of our free institutions".[56]

---

54 Nicolay and Hay, Life of Lincoln Vol. II, p. 357
55 Schouler, History of the *United States*, Vol. V, p. 305
56 Bishop Spalding. Life of Archbishop Spalding, p. 174

In his Essays and Reviews, Brownson spoke of their prejudices as "contemptible"; "The Native-American Party", "is not a party against admitting foreigners to the _rights_ of citizenship, but simply against admitting a certain class of foreigners. It does not oppose _Protestant_ Germans, _Protestant_ Englishmen, _Protestant_ Scotchmen, not even _Protestant Irishmen_. It is really opposed only to _Catholic_ foreigners. The party is truly an anti-Catholic party, and is opposed chiefly to the _Irish_, because a majority of the emigrants to this country are probably from _Ireland_, and the greater part of these are _Catholics_." [57]

By 1856, the Knownothing delegation in Philadelphia nominated as their Presidential candidate Millard Fillmore. The Democratic Party nominated James Buchanan. With the ignoble overwhelming defeat of Fillmore, America had shown her weariness of their tenets and with such the Party evaporated, though only briefly. By 1887 their resurgence came under a new name, The American Protective Association, later the same group called themselves The Ku Klux Clan.

Riots of 1834

* 1/17-27 Irish Labor Riot, Chesapeake and Ohio Canal Williamsport, Md.
* c.3/10 Irish Canal Workers Riot New Orleans, La.

---

57 Brownson, Essays and Reviews, p. 428

* 3/24-26 First Bank of Maryland Riot Baltimore, Md.
* 4/5 Bank of the United States Riot Portsmouth, N.H.
* 4/8-10 Election Riots New York, N.Y.
* c.4/15 Mob Assault on Woman Abusing Slave New Orleans, La.
* 4/22 Whig-Democratic Political Riot Baltimore, Md.
* 4/28 Irish Railroad Workers Riot Mansfield, Mass.
* 6/7 Irish Labor Riot, Chesapeake and Ohio Canal Hagerstown, Md.
* 6/15-24 Irish Riot, Baltimore and Washington Railroad Patuxent, Md.
* c.6/15 Irish Riot, Chenango Canal Chenango, N.Y.
* 7/7-20 Several Anti-Abolitionist Riots New York, N.Y.
* c.June/July Anti-Mormon Riots and "Civil War" Jefferson and Jackson
* Counties, Mo.
* c.7/7 Anti-Abolitionist Riots Newark, N.J.
* 7/9 Anti-Abolitionist Riot Norwich, Conn.
* 8/11-14 Anti-Catholic Convent Riot Charlestown, Mass.
* 8/12-14 Anti-Black Race Riot Philadelphia, Pa.
* c.8/15 Religious Rioting New York, N.Y.
* c.8/20 Stonecutters Labor Riot New York, N.Y.
* c.8/20 Mob Assault on Balloonists Philadelphia, Pa.
* c.9/28 Anti-Irish Riot New York, N.Y.
* c.10/4 Race Riot Columbia, Pa.
* c. 10/4-14 Election Riots Philadelphia, Pa.
* 11/20-22 Irish Labor Riots, Baltimore and Washington Sites between Baltimore Railroad and Washington

Riots of 1835

* 2/13 Rioting between two fire companies Baltimore, Md.
* 2/13 Irish Riot, Chesapeake and Ohio Canal Hagerstown, Md.
* 3/7 German Labor Riot, Baltimore and Between Baltimore
* Washington Railroad and Washington
* c.3/7 Mob assault on woman for alleged prostitution Irville, N.Y.
* c.3/15 Catholic Mob Assault on Anti-Catholic New York, N.Y.
* Protestant Meeting
* Apr.-Aug. Ohio-Michigan Border War Ohio and Mich.
* c.6/21-23 Irish Riots at Five Points New York, N.Y.
* c.7/6 Mob Lynching of Gamblers Vicksburg, Miss.
* c.7/12-15 Irish Riot, Wabash and Erie Canal Indiana
* c.7/13-15 Race Riot Philadelphia, Pa.
* c.7/20 Irish Labor Riot Detroit, Mich.
* c.7/25 Abolitionist Riot to free fugitive slave Albany, N.Y.
* c.8/7 Irish Riots Boston, Mass.
* 8/6-15 Bank of Maryland Riot Baltimore, Md.
* 8/9 Irish-Native Rioting Buffalo, N.Y.
* 8/9 Irish Riot, Chenango Canal Hamilton, N.Y.
* c.8/10 Anti-Abolitionist Riot Lynn, Mass.
* 8/21 Anti-Abolitionist Lynching and Riot Charleston, S.C.
* 8/22 Anti-Abolitionist Riot Boston, Mass.
* 8/31 Anti-Abolitionist and Anti-Free Love Riot Canaan, N.H. against Noyes Academy
* 8/298/29 Race Riot St. Louis, Mo.

* 9/13 Race Riot Washington, D.C.
* c.10/7 Race Riot Forsyth, Ga.
* 10/21 Anti-Abolitionist Riot Utica, N.Y.[58]

QUESTIONS

1. What were the causes for the 'Native American Party?
2. Why were only the Irish Catholics targeted?
3. What was the reasoning for the great fear of a Papal invasion?
4. Explain why the perpetrators were never prosecuted.
5. What gave the Catholic Church the strength to persevere?

---

58   1834 The Great Riot Year, Carl E. Prince, University of Pennsylvania Press Society for Historians of the Early American Republic; *www.jstor.org/stable/3122502*

Index

1. **Saunders, Rev. William.** "Saint Juan Diego and Our Lady." Arlington Catholic Herald catholiceducation.org/articles/stories_of_faith_and.../cs0092.html.
2. **Shea, John Gilmary.** The Catholic Church in Colonial Days. New York : Edward O. Jenkins' & Sons, 1886, pp. 28-88.
3. **Vincent Sasone.** Former Bishops Of Richmond. *The Museum Of Virginia Catholic History and Diocesan Archives.* [Online] September 1, 2010. [Cited: September 1, 2010.] www.richmonddiocese.org/Archives/bishops.htm.
4. **Gallagher, Catholicism in Florida Dr. Charles.**
5. *Fromm, Joseph http://goodjesuitbadjesuit.blogspot.jesuithistory.*
6. www.catholicherald.org/archives/articles. [Online]
7. gosw.abour.com/od/santafenewmexico/ig. [Online]
8. www.newadvent.org. [Online]
9. *www.catholichistory.net/Spotlights/SpotlightFounding.htm.* [Online]
10. *en.wikipedia.org/wiki/Anti-Catholicism.* [Online]
11. Photos, from top: Independence Hall; Boston Massacre; George Rogers Clark's March on Vincennes; John Barry; Flag Raised at Independence Hall. All courtesy of National Archives and Records Administration (unrestricted) , s.l. : s.n.
12. *www.catholichistory.net/people/events.* [Online]
13. **Griffin, Martin I.J.** *Catholics and The Ameriucan Revolution.* 1907.
14. *American Revolution and Aftermath (1776-1800).*
15. *the-american-catholic.com/.../fortnight-for-freedom-day-elelencath...* [Online]

16. *See more at: http://cardinalsblog.adw.org/2012/06/our-first-president-our-first-bishop-and-our-first-freedom/#sthash. XktPlz8Z.dpuf.* [Online]

17. Marian T. Horvat, Ph D. *Let None Dare Call it Liberty: The Catholic Church in Colonial America.*

18. *www.allabouthistory.org/age-of-reason.htm.* [Online]

19. Appletons Encyclopedia. [book auth.] Edited by John Looby. s.l. : Copyright (c) 2001 Virtualology TM.

20. *States and Territories of the United States of America (April 2, 1790 to May 26, 1790) Images of Map of America 1790 bing.com/images.*

21. Bechtle and Metz, p. 243. *Mother Seton.*

22. From a letter to Madame de Barberey-Code. March 25, 1809. Ibid, 152.

23. Marie Celeste, S.C. Elizabeth Ann Seton: A Self-Portrait. Libertyville, Illinois : Franciscan Marytown Press, 1983.

24. Metz, Bechtle and. *Sisters of Charity, Federation of "New Catholic Encyclopdia, 2nd Edition.* Farmington Mills, Michigan : The Gale Group/Thompson Learning Inc, 2003.

25. Br. Silas Henderson, O.S.B. *Saint Elizabeth Seton: Wife, Mother, and Foundress.*

26. Honors Thesis, Gregory Cronin. Burning of the Ursuline Convent. s.l. : Colby College American Studies Department, 1986.

27. *The Great "Riot Year" Jacksonian Democracy and Patterns of Violence in 1834.* Prince, Carl E. 1984, pp. 1-21.

28. www.pahrc.net/index.php/anti-catholicism-jacksonian-philadelphia/huges-john-ca-1861. [Online]

29. Spaulding, J.L. *Life of Archbishop Spaulding.*

30. Hay, Nickolay and. *Life of Lincoln.*

31. www.wikpedia.org. *http://wikpedia.org/wiki/File:Michelangelo's_Pieta-5450-cropncleaned.* [Online]

32. catholicism.org/eight-na-martyrs.html. [Online]

33. *Courtesy of the Special Collections Department, University of South Florida. Digitization provided by the USF Libraries Digitization Center.* [Online]

34. www.paulthigpen.com.

35. Jesuit North American Martyrs -www.wf-f.org/Jesuit_Martyrs.html. [Online]

36. *The Eight North American Martyrs catholicism.org/eight-na-martyrs.html.* [Online]

37. Engh, Mary Jane. *In the Name of Hheaven; 3000 years of religious persecution.* . s.l. : Prometheus Books , 2007.

38. Horvat, Dr. Marian T. *Let None Dare Call it Liberty.*

39. *www.newadvent.org.* [Online]

40. *www.newadvent.org.* [Online]

www.ingramcontent.com/pod-product-compliance
Lightning Source LLC
Chambersburg PA
CBHW072017110526
44592CB00012B/1347